Razormist

//

Does God Love Everyone...
Even a Professional Killer?

DENNIS MCFARLAND

PAGE PUBLISHING, INC.
Conneaut Lake, PA

First originally published by Page Publishing 2021

ISBN 978-1-6624-3141-8 (pbk)
ISBN 978-1-6624-3142-5 (digital)

Printed in the United States of America

CHAPTER LIST

CHAPTER I

A Day in the Life (Part One)

A busy downtown street…

Crowds of people are shuffling through their day. The sidewalks are packed with well-dressed corporate Americans. It is a sunny October day, so it is not unbearably hot. You could say that it is just a "business as usual" kind of day. On one of the busy streets sits a five-star hotel called the Clandestine. A black limo pulls up to the curb and lines up its back doors to the plush red carpet that leads inside. The sunroof over the back section of this stretch is open, and the faint sound of music filters out from within. The windows are tinted deep black so you cannot see the passenger, but the car itself suggests prestige. After just a few moments, five muscle-bound men in expensive suits exit the lobby of the hotel and begin to look up and down the sidewalk. Their actions indicate that they are preparing to escort whoever is in the limo from the car to the hotel lobby.

"Okay, five guards in suits…waiting at the door. Six…seven… counting the two in plain clothes across the street trying to look invisible. The driver inside the limo is most likely armed…and the mark makes nine bodies… Piece of cake…"

One of the muscle-bound guards that came from inside the hotel lobby is momentarily distracted by a gorgeous, slim, dark-haired woman walking toward him on the sidewalk. She is wearing a skintight black dress that comes down to just above her knees. Her hair is long and plush and hangs down past the center of her back. He notices how it gently swings back and forth as she walks. Her stride is subtle but powerful and suggests that she is definitely a professional.

He is momentarily distracted by the fact that she is wearing tennis shoes rather than heels, but he dismisses this crucial detail because he is once again distracted by her beauty. A wicked grin slips over the guard's face as he locks eyes with her. In his mind, he begins to contemplate various compromising positions with her. He awakens from the daydream just in time to see her smiling back at him…with two 9 mm pistols (fitted with silencers) pointed right at him. Her initial attack is so sudden and swift that none of the five men even get a chance to draw their own weapons. Five muscle-bound men in nice expensive suits just simply drop to the ground, dead.

"Nine…eight…seven…six…five…"

Only one of the two plainclothes is sharp enough to see this dark-haired woman quickly cancel out the main guards. As he draws his weapon and looks to alert his partner of the approaching threat… he is just in time to see him fall to the ground. He is just barely missed by the bullet whispering through the air toward him, and he ducks behind a nearby newspaper vending machine. The woman never misses a step in her stride and just merely crouches for cover at the side of the parked limo when she reaches it. With her back against the car, she dumps two empty clips on the ground and pulls the two full ones from their straps high up on her inner thigh.

"Four…"

In what can only be described as a simply astounding display of raw gymnastic ability…the woman leaps into a twisting backflip and lands solid on the roof of the limo, facing the opposite side of the street. In one second, the man pops up over the safety of his newspaper machine to locate the woman he saw moments ago…and she is gone. He quickly ducks down again…waits a second…and pops up again to see if he can see her.

"Three…"

The deadly beauty crosses her arms and drops quickly down through the sunroof and into the car. By now, some passers-by are running for cover. Still others are standing frozen in terror at the scene that has unfolded before them. Although this whole turn of events has only taken seconds to transpire, time seems somehow to warp to a slower pace than humanly possible. The driver door of the limousine pops open, and a dead body falls out onto the street. The man is large, and he makes an audible thump as he hits the ground.

"Two... Where in the heck is the mark?"

From the radio under the dash of the limo, she hears, "MILLER! CODE BLACK! CODE BLACK!" She tosses both guns on the front passenger seat of the limo and prepares to drive away in it. She looks in the direction of the hotel just in time to see the shotgun pointed at her through the passenger-side window. She hears a thunderous sound mixed with the sound of glass breaking as she ducks out the driver-side door. She hears the buckshot rip through the air along with a shower of powdered glass. As she is ducking under the limo to take aim at the two blue snakeskin shoes she sees on the sidewalk across from her, she realizes her guns are inside the car! The feet disappear, and she hears a hollow thump on the hood of the car.

"HEY, MILLER... CODE BLACK, BUDDY!" she shouts from her spot on the ground at the driver side of the limo. She has no idea who this guy is, but she makes the quick-witted comment to try to anger her attacker. Anger clouds the mind, and at this moment, he has the upper hand—perhaps she can hurt his focus a little with her sarcasm. She is calm in spite of the fact that her weapons are inside the limo, and she is in complete control because her mind is sharp as a razor, but at the same time she is thinking, *Where is the mark?*

She gets no response from Miller, but instead, she hears in a solid, booming voice: "FREEZE... POLICE!" She sees a cop on horseback looking back and forth between her and Miller with his gun drawn. Chaos has erupted on the street. Bleeding bodies litter the ground, and panicked bystanders cower into every hidden crevice that offers protection from the conflict. The police sirens are deafening, and in mere seconds, the entire street will be flooded with cops. The cop on the horse shouts, "DROP YOUR WEAPON... NOW!"

She looks back in his direction just in time to see the cop on the horse pitch violently backward in a spray of bone and blood and fall to the ground. A fraction of a second later, through the window of the open car door, she sees Miller jump from the hood of the car to the pavement and land at her side of the limo. In one fluid motion, she sits up and launches herself back inside the open door of the limo. Miller steps around the door and pumps another blast of the shotgun into the front seat. He is frozen for just a fraction of a second with awe—the front seat was empty? He has another mere fraction of a second to think *How is that possible?* and then he sees a wondrous sight. The woman springs out of the sunroof, feet first, and lands squarely on the trunk lid of the limo.

At this moment, as if time itself has stopped completely, Miller sees several things all at once. The horse, having been spooked by the shotgun blast, is streaking down the street as fast as it can in spite of the halted traffic in the immediate vicinity. The first few cop cars are screeching to a halt and forming a perimeter around him and the dark-haired stranger. People are crouching in fear up and down both sides of the street in every little niche that will shield them. Suddenly, the woman leaps off the trunk lid and starts to bolt in the direction of the fleeing horse. She moves with a speed and grace that seems almost supernatural. She zigzags between two newly arriving cop cars and soon is gaining on the horse. He sees her hair flowing rhythmically like a big dark flag waving goodbye to him as she catches up to the fleeing horse. In one swift motion, she leaps onto a nearby car and bounces off it directly into the saddle of the horse. Then she quickly takes the reins of the horse and steers it out of his sight down the nearest side street. Cops are shouting "DROP YOUR WEAPON!" and "GET ON THE GROUND!" all around him. More cop cars are screeching to a halt and building the perimeter around him. He sees all these things, and as time slowly catches up to him, he is hit with a painful realization. He has seen everything but the one thing that would have been the most helpful to him. That crucial detail being the drugged dart that the woman pitched backhanded at him when she leapt from the lid of the trunk. As a wave of unconsciousness overtakes him, and just before he drops to the ground, he thinks, *I hope I see her again!* Then he goes limp and drops to the ground where he was standing, right at the driver side of the limousine.

*****

The horse quickly outlives its usefulness. Just as she rounds the corner, she finds herself face-to-face with an oncoming cop car. Its sirens are wailing loudly. She catches the look of surprise on the officer's face the moment just before impact. At the same time, she bounces up and plants her feet on the horse's saddle. The car is demolished, and the bones of the horse's legs are shattered into powder upon impact. She allows the momentum of the impact to propel her forward over the roof of the cop car. By the time she is able to control her fall and get back on her feet, she is already in a dead run, and she ducks into the nearest alley.

Where the heck *was my mark?* she thinks. *Someone screwed up on their intelligence and almost got me waxed!* She takes a moment to catch her breath and figure out what the next move is. Judging by the sound of the sirens, the police are closing the area in, and she does not have long to get outside the perimeter they are establishing. She hears a shifting nearby and sees a bum crouched in the shadows behind a dumpster a few feet away from where she is standing. It seemed odd to her that with all the commotion that had just erupted a few blocks away this person could somehow be sleeping. She quickly moves closer and sees that that his eyes are definitely relaxed and closed. Although she is a killer, she has always made it a point to not kill innocent people. In the moment, her survival instinct kicks in, and she simply reaches down and snaps his neck. It is clean. It is quick. It is quiet.

The hat, coat, and shoes disgust her. She can feel the stench of the alley like a putrid film over her arms and legs. She also wiped her hands all over the dumpster and wiped some of the grime on her hands and face. As she emerges from the darkness of the alley in her filthy cocoon, she notices two things right away. The first thing is that the police have effectively spread themselves into an ever-widening net, and they are definitely taking this little bit of business seriously. The second thing she sees (which also winds up being the most useful) is that the police have stopped and begun emptying a city bus nearby to search it. This tells her that the cop that collided with the horse she had stolen did not see where she went. She has a few moments to think how lucky she is that in spite of how many cops had flooded into the area and how many people were around, none of them saw her duck into that alley. This turns out to be an unprecedented event of good fortune for her, and she jokingly thinks, *God must be watching over me.* This is sarcasm, of course, because she knows that if there really is a God, he would care nothing for a professional killer. Her thoughts drift momentarily back to William, her adoptive father and one of her trainers, and how much she missed him. He used to try and feed her all that religious crap, and it always seemed to contradict the bulk of other things her training entailed. She has other concerns now though, so she turns her focus back to the issue at hand.

The bus must have been near capacity because there is a rather large group of people on the sidewalk nearby. As she watches, she notices that each person who has been taken off the bus has been given a little white slip of paper. The alley she stepped out of faces directly into the side of a building. To her left, a few cops have parked their cars and are questioning people on the street, and that way led to one of the main intersections, so it is definitely not an option. She sticks to the sidewalk and heads in the direction of the crowd of people being unloaded from the bus. This is still a busy four-way intersection ahead, and the bus is stopped on the opposite corner of the intersection. The police are on high alert, so it is likely that they will remember that she has not gotten off the bus, especially in the rank costume in which she is now cloaked. She is also lacking the little slip of paper that she notices is being handed to everyone getting off the bus. Taking the filthy costume off is also not possible because then she will exactly fit the description of the woman the cops are looking for. If she can get on that bus though, it will be the simplest way of escaping through the perimeter the cops have now firmly established. She can probably get through town in the disguise she is in, but it is a continual risk that anyone who gets close enough to her will see through the stolen clothing and intentional smears of dumpster grease. She slows her pace with a faked drunken stumble in order to buy some more time to survey the surroundings. She decides that the bus is the primary objective, so she mixes with a small crowd of people who are also waiting for the walk signal to flash. There are a few officers standing on the opposite corner directly to her left, a couple of whom are preparing to cross to where she is now standing. Her costume brings with it a helpful side effect in that no one looks her in the eye, and the smell of it keeps people at a distance. The signal changes, and she is now on the same side of the street as the bus. She pauses at this corner now to wait for the signal that will allow her to cross to where the crowd is now reentering the bus. One policeman is talking to the bus driver right at the door of the bus. Two more officers are standing within about a five-foot range of the first one and looking over her and the other commuters. There are officers on all four corners now, and the majority of the crowd has returned to their seats inside the bus. One of the cops looks directly at her, not because he recognized her but because of her disguise and its implications of public intoxication. She keeps her face down, but her eyes are still surveying her surroundings.

The cop standing at the door of the bus with the driver is wearing motorcycle boots, and his pants are tucked into the boots. She gathers from this that his motorcycle must be nearby. As she steps closer to the bus, she sees that the motorcycle is parked right in front of the bus. (In fact, the motorcycle will have to be moved before the bus can pull away.) She can only see the right side of it, just enough to see it is there. She notices a chunk of keys hanging from the cop's belt loop and decides that one of them probably goes to the motorcycle. He is carrying his baton and has a service revolver in his holster as well. He is the oldest of the three officers, so she determines that he must also be the most experienced of the three. (Killing a police officer is never an option because it draws way too much of the wrong attention for a person with her profession. If something happens, it is this experienced officer that will pose the greatest threat to her escape.) She is seven people back in the line of people reentering the bus. She had checked the pockets of the coat she took from the bum and found (surprisingly) that there was a decent amount of bills and some change. She cannot believe her good fortune so far. Of all the bums she could have mugged, she picks the one with money in his pocket. Again, she laughs to herself at the thought of God possibly watching over her. She reaches in the grimy pocket of the coat and counts out the exact amount of bus fare so as not to give the driver enough time to recognize her face. By now, she is five people back in the line. She feels the eyes of the policemen on her and decides that it might look suspicious if she tries to enter the bus without saying anything to them. When she gets to the door of the bus, she fakes a raspy Irish accent and asks, "Are ya acceptin' new passengers on here?" in the general direction of the driver and cop. The two exchange pleasantries, the driver answers "Sure," and steps back onto the bus. The motorcycle cop nods in her direction and turns to walk toward the other two standing nearby. She steps up onto the bus, thinking *Almost home free*, when she hears the walkie-talkies on the cop's hips fire up with "All units, be advised. We have just a found a dead bum in the alley near Spruce and Third. Clothing is missing. Suspect may be disguised in bum's clothing!" In unison, all three cops unsnap their weapon holsters, and the motorcycle cop walks toward the bus, saying "Ma'am…ma'am…" She tries to act as if she does not hear him at first in order to draw him onto the bus, away from the other two, so she steps back into the bus as if she is going to a seat. She gets about four rows back and then turns toward the front of the bus to face the motorcycle cop. He is now standing right next to the driver of the bus, his holster is unsnapped, and his hand is on his weapon. He says to her, "Ma'am, could I have a word with you outside?" She smiles at him, takes a deep breath, and thinks, *So much for the easy escape.*

She has the element of surprise, so she decides to use it. She rushes at the cop and jumps at him full force while at the same time grabbing the hand he is holding his gun with. The pair shatters the front window of the bus and spills out onto the pavement. At the last moment before impact, she draws her knees in so that as they land on the ground, they are driven into his chest. When they land, the breath is knocked out of the cop, which also causes him to reflexively release his hand from his weapon. There was just enough room between the bus and his motorcycle that after landing she can quickly back up against the front of the bus. The most experienced of the three cops is now unconscious on the ground at her feet. She figures he must have also hit his head when they landed, which might leave a nasty bump, but he will live. The two cops who were standing next to the bus both draw their guns and step to the front of the bus. If they had been standing closer together, with one taking a high position and the other taking a low position, they would have been better off. In their excitement and inexperience, they both eagerly step out side by side. Misty rushes toward the gap between them full speed and, the moment she gets there, drops to the ground. As she anticipated, the shock of her movement causes both of them to shoot each other at point-blank range. Both drop to the ground at either side of her with a bullet wound directly in the center of their foreheads. At last count, she recalls that there should be at least four cops in her immediate vicinity. She hears the walkie shout, "SHOTS FIRED! THIRD AND TOWN! SHOTS FIRED, OFFICERS DOWN!"

She quickly runs back and grabs the keys from the belt of the dead motorcycle cop on the ground in front of her and swiftly flips through them. As she anticipated, the make of the motorcycle is printed on the key. She grabs that key off the key ring and slips it into the pocket of the coat. She jumps back against the bus and, with her back to it, begins to slide to the side where the door is. When she and the motorcycle cop burst out the front window of the bus, all the traffic in the vicinity had screeched to a halt from people who had seen the event and stopped to see what was happening. When the first two shots were fired, a few cars had sped up to get out of the line of fire. By this time, traffic had been stopped, and she assumes that all four cops are somewhere near the rear of the bus—and headed her way. She would have to deal with them before she could take off on the motorcycle. She realizes that escape will be impossible in seconds because every officer in the city will be coming right where she is. The bus driver, having somehow come to his senses in the midst of the unfolding drama, begins honking the horn of the bus and shouting "SHE IS AT THE FRONT OF THE BUS!" The passengers are all cowering in their seats, and for the most part, they are quiet.

The motorcycle was the original plan. If she has learned anything over the years she has been a killer, it is to never hesitate. For the gathering number of cops moving toward her position, this is a highly stressful situation. She has the edge because she is calm. There is a high probability that if she can maintain the element of surprise, the cops' aim of their weapons will be off, and she can get away unharmed. She readies the key, takes a deep breath, and leaps onto the seat of the motorcycle.

Two police cars screech into the intersection in front of her and block the road. Two driver's side doors fling open; two cops take cover behind them and begin shooting in her direction. She ducks down, hits the gas, and takes off toward the rear of the bus. Her reflexes are razor-sharp, but so many cops are converging on the area that she knows it will not be long until they close her in—and she can hear a helicopter approaching in the distance. Gunfire erupts all around her, and a few bullets bounce off the bike around her. She sees one bounce off the fuel tank, and for a moment, she wonders if she made the wrong decision jumping on it. Immediately, she looks for the nearest manhole cover so she can ditch it. There is a vast network of sewers and underground tunnels in this city, and she knows once she gets down there, they will never catch her. Just as she thinks this out, a cop car screeches onto the street one block ahead of her and stops. She is going too fast to stop, so the only choice she has is to lay the bike down right in the center of the street.

Time seems to slow down in intense situations. Misty has been trained to utilize those moments and has survived many dangerous encounters precisely because of that training. Several times in the past few months, she had been remembering her adopted father, William. Most of the people involved in her upbringing were trainers and military-type personnel. William was different from all those people, and she dearly misses him. She had been trained to be an emotionless killer, and her love and admiration for William is a secret that she had to lock away deep inside of her. William had a quiet power that she never could understand. Her training brought her into contact with strong and dangerous people, and some of those inadvertently found themselves in William's company along with her. None of them could look William in the eye, and all of them seemed uncomfortable around him. He never talked about his past with her, and she knows very little about him aside from the time he spent with her. She remembers he was a religious man, but he did not fit the traditional stereotype that being religious usually carried with it. He spoke to her several times about God providing and protecting in ways that made God sound like a person William knew. It is the idea of that protection from God that comes to her at this moment as she and the stolen motorcycle slide to a stop in the middle of the street.

A few other things also come to her mind in that moment. The clothing she had taken from the bum in the alley kept her from getting road rash because of crashing the motorcycle. She is in the middle of a daring escape, and there is no way she could have known that the motorcycle accident would happen. She is an experienced professional, but escapes involve adapting to a fluid situation as it unfolds. She took the clothing merely as a disguise, with no possible idea of knowing that it would serve this second purpose as well. She remembers William telling her that God has a plan and that there is no such thing as coincidence, so she laughingly wonders if God placed that bum in the alley for her benefit because he knew the clothing she stole would protect her in this moment. It is the sound of bullets whistling by her and around the motorcycle that shockingly brings her back to the present moment.

She plants her hand on the ground to rise up enough that she can assess her situation. She feels a small hole in the street under one of her fingers and is shocked to see that by some crazy stroke of pure luck, she and the motorcycle have come to rest right on top of a sewer lid in the middle of the street. She cannot help but laugh to herself as she flips the sewer lid to the side and jumps down into the subterranean safety it offers. She is not out of the woods yet, but with the confusion she created aboveground, her escape is sure now. The sewer is cool and damp and smells terrible. The tunnel is not large enough for her to stand up in, so she has to crouch and run to get away. She waits until nightfall to exit the sewer tunnel and climbs out under the cover of night two blocks from where she left her vehicle. The vehicle is stolen, and once she gets out of the city, she will just abandon it in the next one. She took it just hours before doing this job, so by the time they find it, there is no way they will connect it to her.

The job...

The mark was not in the limo when it pulled up out front of the Clandestine. She had disabled all the security cameras earlier the night before, so there was no danger in that. Several people had seen her, though, because she was unable to drive away in the limo. Everything happened so fast that it is not likely anyone got a good look at her. The police will have plenty of conflicting descriptions to keep them busy. She does not know who Miller is, and he is not in any of the intelligence that was given to her when she accepted the assignment.

CHAPTER 2
The Living Room

The small girl waited silently in the darkness and tried to listen for any sound that might be helpful. The silence was deafening. Inside, she knew he was in here with her somewhere, but she had all her plans in place. Now all she had to do was wait.

She felt so vulnerable in this vast open blackness. At the same time, she was determined to prove to him that she had learned the lessons he had drilled into her. At just nine years old, she had endured more physical and emotional training than most adults could handle. She had never known anything different, and for as long as she could remember, she had been in training. There were two men given charge of her training. William, the one she loved, was more of a father figure to her. He was a large quiet man, but he had a kind smile, and she always had a good time with him. The other, Mr. Casey, was mean, and he was in this room with her somewhere.

This day's training took place in what was called the "living room." She was brought here once a week for this exercise. She had a few moments to memorize the details of the room and then find the perfect place to set an ambush before the lights were turned off. The point of this exercise was that she had to knock Mr. Casey down in a way that it was hard for him to get back up. The living room was fully furnished like a living room you might find in a typical upscale home. There was a big plush couch that sat about one and a half feet high on ornate wooden legs. In one of the earlier training sessions, she had tried to crawl under it and hide to trip him. The hard kick to the belly she received taught her quickly to not go to the most obvious place.

There were two plush high-backed chairs with a table between them. These also sat upon ornate wooden legs. There was a table lamp sitting on the center of the table, but she was not sure if it worked. There was a coffee table that sat directly in front of the couch. There were magazines spread across the top of the coffee table, but she had never gotten a glance of the titles before the lights went out. She just knew they were there. There were two fully stocked bookshelves in the room as well. In a different previous training session, she had armed herself with a few of the books to throw at Mr. Casey, hoping to knock him off-balance. In the darkness, it was difficult to get a solid shot at him. After launching the first one at him, he quickly dodged the others or swatted them aside. She had gotten a rare word of praise from him for her resourcefulness but was sent to bed without dinner for failing once again to subdue him.

There were various knickknacks placed on the small table and the coffee table, as well as various ones on a few of the bookshelves. She had considered all these as weapons at one time or another but had dismissed them as equally ineffective as the books she had once tried. The living room had caused her a considerable amount of stress, and she had many sleepless nights pondering how to subdue Mr. Casey so she could stop having to train in there. The answer came to her as the result of three distinct but unrelated events. Each event had no significance with each other, and it wasn't until the last of three had occurred that her mind was able to put them together as a solution to the "living room" problem.

The first event took place in the cafeteria. It was a large room, and the only cafeteria in the facility as far as she knew. She was the only child there, and other than Mr. Casey and William, none of them paid any attention to her. The food was good there, and she spent most of her mealtimes swinging her legs back and forth and looking out the window. She was given time to play outside regardless of the weather, but the majority of her time outside was for training. This particular day, she was thinking about the word "training." She knew that the games and exercises she did every day were called training, but she had no idea what the word meant. She had figured out that her training was getting her ready for something, but she did not know what that thing might be. She thought a lot about the different games and exercises, each element of them, and what they might have in common. The living room, in particular, kept her mind occupied a great deal. Mr. Casey did not hit her hard, but he did strike her hard enough to make her sore. He explained it by saying, "The pain will help you remember not to repeat your mistakes." Most of the time, she was not sure what the mistakes were in the moment, but Mr. Casey always sat her down to tell her after she had been struck.

As she was eating and thinking, she noticed a lady getting ready to sit at one of the tables nearby to eat her lunch. The lady was tall and had her hair pulled back into a ponytail. There were some magazines sitting on the table, and as the lady sat down and placed her tray on the table, a couple of the magazines slipped off onto the floor. At the same time, a man was walking by to throw away his trash. The man was looking back toward the place he had just gotten up from and talking to another guy as he walked. He did not see the magazines fall on the floor in front of him. She saw it register in the tall lady's eyes that the man was going to step on them and that she was getting ready to say something. Before she could, the man stepped on the magazines and slipped on them. His tray and trash went flying and made a big mess. He was not seriously injured though, and after picking up as much of the mess that he could, he left the cafeteria. She was lost in thought, and in the moment, she did not realize that the first part of the solution for the living room had just happened right in front of her.

She loved William. He was her teacher, and she looked forward every day to school time with him. He was a big muscular man, but he spoke very quietly. What she liked most about his lessons was the way he used everyday examples to explain things in ways she could understand. The second event took place during lesson time with William. It was knowledge she gained concerning how electricity worked. What she remembered from the lesson, as William had explained it, was that electricity moves through wires kind of how water moves through pipes. In the same way that a broken pipe will let water come out, a broken wire lets electricity out. The main difference is that electricity was much more dangerous. It could burn you really badly and even kill you. He explained that turning switches on and off was kind of like turning water on and off. This was all very interesting to her, and she spent the next couple days after that lesson considering the flow of electricity all around her. It was this contemplation that caused to think of the lamp on the table in the living room. Maybe if there was electricity going into that lamp, she could use it somehow to her advantage?

She was excited for the next time she was trained in the living room. She needed to find out if there was electricity going to that lamp, but she wanted to make sure that Mr. Casey didn't notice her checking it out. It was very frustrating to her that he seemed to be able to know right where she was every time. She was careful to never say what she was thinking about the room, but he was so quick to find her most of the time that she really started to believe he could read her thoughts. She had already decided to try and push one of the bookshelves over on top of him the next time they were in the room when she thought he was close to her, but she didn't know how heavy it was. Going into the room this time, she made it a point to make her way quickly to where the bookshelves were and wait quietly there to listen for him. In the quiet, she thought she heard the faint sound of footsteps approaching her. Right at the moment she thought he was in front of her, she wedged her hand between the nearest shelf and the wall and started to push it over. She had to reposition her hand once for better leverage, but she finally managed to topple it over. A few moments after the racket from the shelf being knocked over had died down, Casey called for the lights to be turned back on. She was shocked to see him standing right next to her.

"Now why did you do that?" he asked.

She was frustrated again by the fact that he once again seemed to know right where she was. The bookcase was, of course, a distraction for what she really wanted to do in the living room today. She concentrated hard to not think about or picture that lamp in her mind just in case he could somehow read her thoughts—she wasn't sure. She was very careful with her reply.

"I waited until I thought I heard you standing in front of it, and then I tried to push it over on top of you to knock you down."

He asked her, "So were you sure I was standing in front of it when you pushed it over? Did you know exactly where I was in the room?"

"No, sir, Mr. Casey," she replied.

"The bookcase is a good idea, but only if you can be sure a person is standing in front of it, right?" he asked. She nodded her head in agreement. This was the first time he had acknowledged an idea of hers as good concerning the living room, but she had not successfully subdued him, so she wondered what the punishment was going to be. His next words were a shock to her: "Pick the bookcase back up, and put everything back on it neatly the way it was. Then go eat."

She smiled and nodded again as he left the room, surprised that there would be no punishment this time. She noticed something in his hand as he walked out of the room but could not make out what it was. It wasn't important for now, so she dismissed it. The bookcase was heavy, and it took her a few minutes to stand it back up and scoot it back to where it belonged. She placed all the books and knickknacks back on the shelves and turned to leave the room. As she was walking out of the room, she stopped briefly in front of the small end table placed between the two chairs. She reached over and turned the small plastic knob to see if the lamp would turn on. It did. She quickly turned it back off and smiled widely as she left the room. Her plan began to form, but there was one last element she needed to fall into place that would solidify a solution for her concerning the living room. That last event took place in the late evening on the same day.

It was storming that evening when she headed back to her room for the night. She was thinking about the living room and how to use her newfound knowledge of electricity in the situation. Just as she was opening her door to enter her room, there was a loud crash of thunder, and the lights in the facility went out. The emergency lights randomly placed throughout the hall came on soon after, but her room was still dark as she walked in. She paused for a moment to let the shock from the crack of thunder to pass and then walked into her room.

Earlier in the day, she had been reading some of her favorite books on the floor of the room. When she was called away, as she typically did, she just left them lying on the floor. In the excitement of the day, and with her mind buzzing about plans for the living room, she had forgotten about the books lying open on the floor in the pool of darkness. She stepped on one of them, and her foot slipped out from underneath her. She fell to the floor and skinned her elbow slightly on the carpet. She collected her thoughts in the moment and remembered the books she had left on the floor. Immediately after that, she remembered the man slipping on the magazines in the cafeteria. She somehow mentally connected these two moments with the small stack of magazines on the coffee table in the living room, and her plan began to form. There was still the possibility that he could somehow read her thoughts, she needed to figure out how he was able to anticipate her plans before she could put this new plan forming in her young mind into action. As she lay quietly in her bed that night in the darkness, she started thinking deeply about how to finally beat Mr. Casey in his own living room. Her thoughts went back over that day's exercise, and she remembered briefly that he had something in his hand as he walked out that day. After thinking about it further, she remembered a few other times noticing something in his hand as they walked out of the room. She was not sure how this had escaped her before. The storm continued through the night, both outside as well as in her mind.

The next couple times she was given the living room exercise, it seemed to Mr. Casey that she was not even trying. She was sent to her room those two evenings without dinner. This was fine with her because she was actually using the time to lay her secret plan. Each time, at the close of the exercise, she noticed Casey was indeed holding something. He seemed to be concealing it in whatever hand was on the opposite side of his body from where she was standing. At the close of the next exercise, she demanded to see what it was he was holding.

Casey was shocked at first that she had noticed it and tried to play it off like he didn't know what she was talking about. She insisted and added that this was not the first time she had seen him carrying something out of the room. He had to admit that he had underestimated her powers of observation and that he was slightly impressed. This also proved that she had been considering these observations outside of when she was participating in the exercise. He finally relented and handed her what he was holding.

It was a strange object unlike anything she had ever seen before. It seemed like a ball cap, except it had what looked like a small telescope attached to the front of it. She rolled it around in her hands for a few moments, trying to figure out what it was. She finally gave up and asked him about it. "What is this thing?"

Mr. Casey smiled and answered, "It is a night vision goggle. It makes it so I can see in the dark."

All at once, she was extremely angry but at the same time super happy. She finally knew that it was not some kind of mind-reading power but that he was simply cheating. Her mind raced over all the previous times she had done the living room exercise, and now she understood how it was so easy for him. More importantly, she knew in this moment how to execute the plan she had been working on for the past couple weeks. In fact, she knew she could beat him.

"THAT'S NOT FAIR!" she shouted.

Casey tried to redirect the conversation toward the fact that sometimes others will have advantages over her, and he used his famous "You need to learn to adapt and overcome" speech he typically turned to. She wasn't having any of that. She chose her next words very carefully. Her mind was clear, but she knew that things had to be perfect if her plan was going to work. She expected Mr. Casey to underestimate her as well; she was actually counting on it. She calmed herself and spoke clearly and carefully. "You spent a lot of time putting the living room together to make it as real as possible… right?"

Casey nodded his head in approval.

"Whatever it is I am supposed to be learning, that also needs to be as real as possible…right?"

Casey again nodded his head in agreement.

"Well, real people cannot see in the dark! If you plug in that lamp and walk over to it in the dark to turn it on, I *bet* I could *get you* before you could even turn that light on!"

It was out. She watched his face to see if she could figure out how he was going to respond. She knew he could not read her mind now, and she knew if he accepted this challenge, she had him right where she wanted him to be. The few seconds it took for him to respond seemed like an eternity.

"Is that a challenge, Misty?" he finally asked.

She had him! She pushed her shoulders back and stared him right in the eye and replied, "No, that is a promise." With that, she turned and walked away. As she walked away, she heard Casey reply, "Okay, kid, you're on."

Casey was amazed at her intelligence. He had seen a confidence in her eyes that he had never seen before. He had been training Special Forces soldiers for several years and was reluctant to accept a job training a small child. What he saw in her eyes in that moment made him smile, and he wondered what idea she had cooked up in her little mind. At first, he was going to continue using the goggles, but after some thought, he decided she was just a child—what real harm could she really do? He was completely unprepared for the ferocity of the attack she had prepared.

She could hardly wait until the next time she was called for the living room exercise. She was jumping up and down excitedly outside the door to the room, waiting to be let in and start. The light in the hall outside the room went out first to signify the beginning of the exercise. The door to the room opened, and as usual, she walked in and let the door shut and lock behind her. The lights in the living room remained on for thirty seconds and then cut off. She immediately sprang into action as soon as the lights went out. She had no idea how long she would have before Casey entered the room. She had spent the last few times in the room pacing out some dimensions to be sure she could do it quickly. When she was sure everything was in place, she waited quietly behind the table with the lamp on it.

She carefully pulled the wire loose from the bottom of the lamp and separated the ends of the wire as she waited.

Casey entered the room from a separate entrance than the one the girl entered from, but it was on the same wall. He wore soft-soled shoes and crept silently toward the lamp. He took time to go the long way around the couch, figuring she might be poised in the darkness in the immediate path to the light from the door. She had boasted that she could get him "before he could even turn the light on." He had memorized the layout of the room and had come in alone a couple times to pace out the dimensions of the room himself. He smiled secretly to himself when he arrived at the lamp and reached out to turn it on.

The moment his hand grasped the small knob to turn the lamp on, he felt a sharp burning sensation on the back of his hand that caused him to immediately jerk his hand back. It did not register immediately what had happened. A second later he felt the same sharp burning sensation on the front of his leg, and then the same thing on his other leg. The surprise of the pain caused him to instinctively take a step back away from the table. When he did, he stepped onto the stack of open magazines she had strategically scattered in that spot on the floor. He lost his footing and fell to the floor. As he was falling, he found that the coffee table was at an odd angle. He figured she might be pushing it toward him, so he rolled to the far side of it to try and regain his footing. She had shifted the coffee table in anticipation of his fall and did so to direct him right where she wanted him to be. It took a second for him to get his bearings and realize where he was in the room. Of course, he was a moment too late. Immediately after shocking him on the hand and legs with the exposed wire from the lamp, she had moved around the perimeter of the room and positioned herself momentarily beside that first bookshelf. She heard him fall in the darkness and bump into the coffee table exactly where she had placed it. Now she knew he was in place, and she pushed the bookshelf down right on top of him.

There was a deafening silence in the room after everything had settled. She stood quietly against the wall, waiting to see what Casey would do, but she knew she had got him. She knew he had underestimated her, and she wondered for a brief second in that silence if she had hurt him. From the floor, Casey erupted into a fit of laughter like she had never heard before. It lasted long enough that she could not help but chuckle a little bit herself. Between bursts of laughter, he called for the lights to be turned on.

He was lying on the floor, still under the bookcase, covered in books and knickknacks, with tear streaks down his cheeks. He pushed the shelf off and stood up. She could see the two small burn marks on the legs of his black jumpsuit where she had zapped him with the exposed wires. She was still unsure what was going to happen, but for a few minutes she laughed uneasily with him.

After a few more minutes, his laughter had calmed, and he said, "*That* was *awesome*, Misty!" He walked over to the small table and looked behind it to see the exposed lamp cord lying on the floor against the wall. He looked back over to where she was standing and said, "Of course…the lamp cord…nice touch." He crossed his arms on his chest and looked around the room. He had really underestimated her level of intelligence. He had mistaken her challenge as childish boasting, but now in this moment, he realized that it was more than that. She had made a plan and executed the plan with perfection. She knew what the outcome was going to be when she issued that challenge. He decided in that moment that he was going to have to start being more careful when training her.

He added, "See, the bookshelf is much more effective when you are sure the person is in front of it." She smiled and nodded in his direction. She had rarely seen Mr. Casey smile like this. He was a hard and serious man, and she had gotten used to seeing him that way. It was a little unnerving to see him like this, and she realized in that moment that her relationship was going to be different from now on with him. She was ready to explode on the inside because she knew that whatever the lesson of the living room was, she had learned it, and it was over.

Casey said, "Someone else will clean this up. Go get changed and cleaned up… I have a treat for you." She had no idea what the treat was, but the fact that Mr. Casey was the one treating motivated her to quickly exit the room to go change and clean up. She nearly knocked William over in the hallway as she left the room. She hollered a greeting to him and continued on toward her quarters. William entered the room and made eye contact with Casey. "Well?" he asked.

Casey shook his head and said, "I had my doubts about training a child, but not anymore."

Casey took a few moments to explain to William about the plan Misty had executed, and they both discussed the implications of what that meant concerning the direction of her training. For different reasons, neither man agreed with the idea of training an assassin at such a young age. The games and exercises they engaged her in were made to seem like just that. She was way too young to fully understand the concept of life and death. There was no way either man was going to try to explain to her at this age that she was actually being trained to kill people. Originally, both men had doubts that a child could act with the dangerous animosity of a trained killer. Now, both men were forced to reconsider that thought. Granted, she had no idea what the ultimate purpose of the living room was, but that did not take away from the ability she showed in turning the environment into something dangerous to suit her purposes.

The training facility was in a remote location, and while she was allowed to play outside from time to time, she was never taken off-site. She had not been denied the occasional treat from the outside world though. She loved McDonald's french fries just like any other kid her age. She, of course, kept the toys that came with the Happy Meals she had been given.

Now she had crossed a milestone in her training. William and Casey both felt it was appropriate to mark this event with a special treat. To maintain an acceptable level of psychological development, it was necessary that one of the two be the authority figure, and the other be the father figure. While Casey actually wanted to be the one to take her, he understood that it was William's place. Both men walked her outside to a waiting jeep, but Casey spoke first.

"Misty, you did a fantastic job today in the living room. I am truly impressed with what you did in there. You made your plan, and you executed that plan just like I taught you. We will be doing some more games and exercises from now on, but you are done with the living room. Nicely done." She looked back and forth at both men wondering what treat she had earned.

Casey smiled at both of them and then walked back into the facility. She was busting at the seams inside, and she looked up at William to see what was going on. He looked down at her, smiled, and said, "Well, what are you waiting for? Get in."

William drove her into the nearest town and took her into McDonald's for the first time ever. He could not help but smile as he watched her drink in the sights and sounds. She had never been off the grounds before. She sat in the booth, kicked her feet, and happily devoured her meal in silence while taking in the sights and sounds around her. He chuckled momentarily to himself with the thought that in many senses, this was truly a happy meal. They sat and talked for a while there, and Misty was full of questions. He listened to her excitedly tell him about how she developed the plan that she executed in the living room, and it was a great evening for both of them that neither one would ever forget.

She had a real sense that something had changed. This was the first time she had ever been taken off the grounds of the facility. She loved being at McDonald's, and she could not contain the excitement of seeing three dimensional statues of characters she had only seen printed on the boxes of her happy meals. There were so many people here. Not just the ones in McDonald's with her and William, but all around. She looked at each face and wondered what the stories were that went with each one. There was so much noise and activity in the world, and she drank in as much of it as possible.

William was enjoying her wide-eyed amazement so much that he intentionally took the long way back to the facility to give her as much time as possible to take it all in. It was a bittersweet moment for him. He knew that the path she was on led to pain, solitude, and darkness. She was being molded into a coldhearted killer, but in this moment, he just could not bring himself to accept that thought.

Mr. Casey was waiting outside for them when they returned. She hugged both men and skipped off to her quarters with her Happy Meal box and new toy in hand. William and Casey briefly discussed how her first trip to the outside world had turned out, and they then parted company. William was troubled the more he thought about the future awaiting Misty, and he prayed that night that she would develop an inner peace that would carry her through the difficult times that were sure to come. He had a long and distinguished career in the military, but he did not agree with most of the secrets his position had brought him exposure to. In this moment, he decided that he could not, with a clear conscience, continue to participate in a program where this beautiful little girl was being trained to be a killer.

Misty had no idea that this was the last day she would ever see William. She merely collapsed in her bed without even changing into pajamas and slept more soundly that night than she had in a long time.

Chapter 3
Crystal's Story

It is a hot and miserable day to be homeless.

The heat rises in waves from the pavement of the hot city streets. The air is heavy, and each breath is an effort. In the afternoon sun, with the heat shimmering off every surface nearby, it almost seems as if she is actually walking underwater. The world goes about its daily business, unaware of the mixture of anger and sorrow burning within her. The heat of the day only feeds her anguish at the situation in which she has found herself. As she slowly shuffles through the downtown streets, her thoughts go back to how the whole thing started.

*****

She was anxiously awaiting her twenty-first birthday. Her parents were strictly religious people, and the rules of her home life were so restricting that she moved out the day of her eighteenth birthday determined never to go back. All her friends were slightly older and had been partying for a while. She would still drink with them from time to time, but she could not get into the exclusive clubs they attended on the nights they decided to go out. She lived with two other girls and worked as a waitress to cover her portion of the bills. It was a small apartment, so with the bills split three ways, there was always plenty of money left for drugs and alcohol. She seemed to be so free in those days, and a smile breaks briefly across her sweaty face as she remembers the good times she seemed to be having. All three girls were attractive, so there were always plenty of people who wanted to come by the apartment and hang out.

She took the day of her birthday off in anticipation of an entire day and evening of getting high and drunk with her friends. She was young, she was attractive, and she was finally old enough to go to the places she had always wanted to get into. She felt invincible. The one club she decided she wanted to go to was called Encounters. There were many neon lights on the front of the building, and the beat of the music emanating from inside the open doors seemed to have a hypnotic effect on her. She slid into her tiny black dress, put on her makeup, and jumped in the back seat of her friend's convertible that evening prepared for the night of her life. She had no idea that her life would change forever that night and of the suffering she would soon endure.

The bouncer at the entrance to Encounters was the largest man she had ever seen. She smiled at him in spite of her nervousness because of his size as she handed him her ID. He wished her a happy birthday and smiled briefly at her as he stepped aside to let her in. She remembered thinking as she passed by him that he must be made of rock, steel, or some other substance besides human flesh. The lights and music immediately grabbed her attention though, and she stopped for a quick second to breathe deeply of the atmosphere in the club. Her friends patted her on the back and headed straight to the dance floor. She decided that she wanted to go to the bar first and purchase her first drink to celebrate being twenty-one at last.

*****

It seems so long ago to her today. She misses Angela and Nicole, and she wonders what they might be doing in life right now. She wonders if they ever think about her. It has been nearly ten years ago, and that was the last time she saw them—as they walked away from her that night, headed to the dance floor. The smile fades from her face, and for a moment, the heat of the day seems to drain a little more from her than it already had.

*****

The bartender looked her up and down when she stepped up to the bar. He also wished her a happy birthday as he handed her the celebratory drink. The first one was on the house, and it was the last thing she remembered from that night.

Her dad was a Baptist minister. He had been a man of the Word her whole life. She had heard his testimony more times than she could count that prior to his walk he had been an atheist. He was a very controlling man. As soon as she was able to read and understand the scriptures for herself, she continued to struggle with her father's teachings. She read of the love, grace, and freedom provided by her Heavenly Father in the Bible, she but could not find it in the cruel religious restriction imposed on her family by her earthly father. She remembered looking at old pictures of her mother when she was younger. Her mother was beautiful and vibrant back then, but the years of strict adherence to their religion had quenched the fire that once burned in her to a mere spark.

She was close to her mother and felt loved by her. Although she would never admit it, she believed her mother secretly longed for an escape from her life, but that she extracted joy and satisfaction from her relationship with her daughters. Crystal decided from an early age never to be captive to the religious restriction she saw sucking the life and vitality out of her mother. She saw her dad as the source of that religious restriction, and for as long as she could remember, she resented him for it. She loved her dad but only out of a sense of responsibility to do so. She never felt a connection to him, and she never felt a connection from him. Inevitably, Crystal had to learn to suppress her independent spirit, but often she found herself in conflict with her dad because of it. His punishment was always biblically justified, and his judgment and decisions were always final. He was never to be questioned, and his interpretation of the scriptures was the final authority on all things.

She had an older sister and a younger sister. Deborah, the oldest, was always the good child. She despised Deborah because she could never understand why she so easily embraced Dad's rules and regulations. She used to call Deborah "Parrot Head" and take every opportunity to poke fun at her for being daddy's little girl. Her dad made all the children learn to play a musical instrument. Deborah played the piano, and she was very good at it. Crystal learned to play the flute. It was not because she had any interest in it. It was merely because she knew she had to pick something, and the flute seemed like the simplest thing to learn. She figured she would never pick it up again after she moved out. Lydia, the youngest sister, played the violin. Their dad considered their musical performances part of the family ministry, which was a mandatory part of the rules of the household. She hated to admit it because she was forced to learn the instrument, but she was actually very talented on the flute. Deborah was the pride of the family's music ministry, and Crystal was always jealous of the extra love and attention she received as a result. Deborah was not an innocent victim in the relationship. Deborah was manipulative. Crystal found herself spanked—and as she got older, grounded—many times because of Deborah's manipulation of their dad. That manipulation also worked itself out concerning distribution of the family finances as well. Because Deborah was the star of the show, her wardrobe was more lavish and larger than her two sisters' combined were. While this never seemed to bother Lydia, it meant continual conflict between Deborah and Crystal.

Crystal always thought of her little sister Lydia as the flower of the family. She was the baby of the family, and everything she did seemed cute. She could not allow herself to be mad or jealous toward Lydia for an extended amount of time. Lydia was blessed because she was beautiful and because she had an innocent honesty about her that immediately endeared people to her. She embraced the religious restrictions of the household as a fact, and they never seemed to bother her. Deborah was jealous of Lydia but could not bring herself to turn their parents on her in the same way she did to Crystal. She usually eyed Lydia distastefully but would fake a smile when Lydia said or did something worthy of it. Lydia was blissfully ignorant when it came to Deborah's character flaws. She could only see the apparent glamour and recognition Deborah received. Lydia called her Princess Deborah, and although she did not mean it with any kind of malice, Crystal laughed inside every time Lydia called her that. Lydia was too young, in Crystal's opinion, to learn to play a musical instrument. She played the violin reasonably well for her age, and she was so cute that when she missed a note, it seemed like such a precious thing, nobody really cared. Crystal wanted to be jealous of the fact that Lydia looked up to Deborah instead of her, but she could not be. She knew Lydia loved her and missed the random hugs she would get from time to time that proved it.

*****

The heat of the afternoon intensifies, and breathing becomes so difficult that it brings Crystal out of her daydreaming. It is a wet heat, and it seems to form a liquid film on every surface around her. People walking the streets look as if they were wading down the sidewalk rather than walking. Their dragging pace makes it seem as if the heat of the day has combined with the natural force of gravity, making every step seemingly more difficult. The good thing about the heat is that it keeps people distracted, so she was relatively unnoticed. She had learned to ignore the looks of distaste passersby would cast in her direction. She hates herself for what she has become, and those looks of distaste only feed her growing lack of self-confidence. She has to keep running and hiding. It is not safe to put down any roots because if she does, there is a chance that Julius will find her. She is unwilling to take that risk. Her only option is to keep moving, so after a brief pause to catch her breath, she pushes on into the blazing hot streets, trapped inside herself.

*****

She knew very little about the guy her dad was before he committed his life to God. She had heard him say several times that he was a former atheist, but beyond that, he rarely shared about his past. It seemed strange to her, in fact, that he seemed to have erased his past, as if he had no life prior to his relationship with God. There were no pictures in the house from his childhood or teenage years. There were no pictures of her mother and him from when they started dating. A few times, she had asked her mother what kind of person he was before, but her mother would change the subject, seemingly out of fear that her dad did not want the story told. He talked down to everyone but elders of the church or people whose relationships seemed advantageous to him. There were times when Crystal wanted to scream to everyone that he was not the same person at home that he was in public. Her dad portrayed her as the troublemaker though, so the majority of the people in their social circles would just dismiss it as rebelliousness. The thing Crystal remembered most about her dad, the thing that came immediately to the forefront of her thoughts when she thought of him, was the wild zealous look in his eyes. It was intimidating to her, and it was such a part of him that she was sure that other people had to be intimidated by it as well. It was as if a religious fire was burning in his soul that made him an instrument of God's wrath. It was not the love or the grace or the mercy of God in his eyes—it was always the judgment and the wrath that shined from within him. The judgment and wrath of God permeated every part of his being. It was in his actions as he dealt with the people around him, and everything he said, no matter what, was somehow peppered with those angry elements.

She never felt or sensed love or any other kind of connection to her dad. At best, she felt like a tool he used to accomplish whatever he believed God's work was. He would make time for her, but it usually seemed as if he was only doing it out of a sense of biblical responsibility to do so. He was cold and impersonal, and the few times he tried to project any kind of lovingness, which was usually in the company of others, it never seemed to be genuine. The majority of her childhood and teenage years were made up of being under some kind of punishment or being lectured on proper biblical behavior. She learned, painfully at times, that the best thing to do was keep her mouth shut and endure until the time was right to move out.

Talking back only made the lectures and punishment worse.

*****

This last statement gives her pause. In a sudden rush of grief, she is awakened from the daydreams of her past life and the reality of her situation. The heat of the day seems to intensify. She has not eaten a solid meal in two days. The few scraps she could normally pick from the local dumpsters spoil too quickly in the summer heat. Her stomach growls like a starving animal and adds to the misery and torment she feels. She had overheard a conversation about a local church passing out meals to the homeless the previous night. She decides to go check it out. The thought of having to listen to another speech about how she can turn to Jesus in her time of need makes her cringe, but her hunger motivates her to go get the food in spite of it. Her thoughts return to the statement she was contemplating before her stomach growled in protest.

*****

The last thing she remembered from her birthday celebration at Encounters was the free drink she received at the bar. That was partially true. She had other foggy memories of dancing and lights and music, but that first drink was her last clear memory from that night. As hard as she tried, she could not remember meeting Julius. She does not remember seeing him at Encounters. She does not remember leaving Encounters. All she remembers is that free drink and then waking up to a nightmare that lasted nearly ten years of her life.

She awakened bound and gagged in a room that looked like a jail cell. The walls were waterproof, sealed with thick white paint. There were no windows though, which seemed as strange to her then as it does now. There was one heavy wooden door with several locks on it and a gray metal folding chair in the center of the room. The room had a high ceiling, and a single light bulb with a pull chain dangled loosely in the middle of the room. In one corner, there was a stainless steel toilet and a sink mounted to the wall. She was instantly terrified upon awakening in this room, and she immediately started trying to break free from the ropes that bound her. She struggled seemingly for hours against those ropes, but all she got was rope burn and discouragement as she finally fell back in an exhausted heap. She remembers having this extreme sense of dread and thinking that this room was only the beginning of what was to come. She renewed her struggles once again but was not able to break free. She had no sense of time since she woke up in that room, but she knew it was several hours before that heavy wooden door opened and the real nightmare began. By that time, her ankles and wrists were raw and bloodied, and she was very exhausted. She still wonders if it would have mattered had she relaxed and saved her strength that day, and if she could have escaped. That day was so long ago, and compared to the horrors she endured afterward, she decides it really does not matter. A tear escapes her eye as she remembers the young woman who was lost that day.

She first met Julius in that terrible room. He was dressed in blue jeans and a red polo shirt. His hair was pulled back into a ponytail. He was not a very big person, but he was muscular. His teeth were white as snow, and his smile reminded her of a great white shark. He entered the room, locked the doors behind him, and positioned the chair so he could see her before he sat down in it. He had her purse in his hands. She remembered feeling violated as he looked through it right in front of her. He pulled out her wallet and looked at her driver's license briefly. He put all the contents back in it and set the purse on the floor beside him. She was terrified, but now, she remained silent to see what was going to happen next. He crossed his arms and spoke very softly to her.

"My name is Julius. From now on, your name is Lisa. You will do what I say when I say it, and you will not question me. Talking back to me in any way will only make your punishment worse. You have no family. You have no history before this room. I will kill anyone you contact. You belong to me now. This is going to be your life from now on. Do you understand?"

Crystal began sobbing heavily, and she desperately hoped that this was some kind of joke. She searched his eyes for some kind of mercy, some glimmer of hope, but found none. She could not help herself and began sobbing even more heavily. Julius shifted slightly in his chair and said softly to her, "You have thirty seconds to stop crying."

Some place deep within her hoped that her tears would inspire some kind of sympathy. She did not believe till this moment that such cruelty existed in the world. She longed for home, she missed her friends, and she had never known or been exposed to the possibility of savagery she had currently encountered. Julius did not count the thirty seconds aloud. He just calmly peered down at his wristwatch until the time had run out. Being careful not to damage her face, he attacked her with such brutality that when he was finished, Crystal was sure that death was certain. He left her in that room, bruised and battered, for two weeks. She was given one meal a day and told that she would "work them off" as soon as the bruises faded.

That was how the ordeal began for her. Because she was young and beautiful, many men requested her company from Julius. They paid large sums of money to do things with her of such depravity that words simply cannot express. The only rule Julius had concerning his girls was that no damage could be done to their faces. Any other manner of torture or depravity was acceptable, provided no serious damage was done that would kill them or render their services useless. On occasion, a client would get too rough with one of the girls, resulting in their accidental death. In such cases, the client would be charged an outrageous fee, which they would gladly pay to keep from having to deal with the alternative consequences. Julius had seven girls "working" for him. He kept a relatively small clientele and hardly ever accepted new clients. He made enough money to live a comfortable life but not a lavish enough lifestyle to be noticed by the authorities. He kept no records, either written or computerized, and made all his business deals verbally. He only accepted cash and never kept a bank account. He paid cash up front for everything he had and signed no contracts or other financially oriented paperwork.

Each of the girls occupied their own cell in a soundproofed underground bunker. The soundproofing was so effective that Julius joked with his clients that a bomb could go off in one of those cells and you would not know if you were in the one next to it. The bunker was built in the basement of his home. He kept them down there until each of them were docile enough to be trusted with roaming free in his home without worrying that they would attempt escape. He never spent time with the girls—in fact, he actually felt contempt and distaste for them. They were dirty to him, and besides beating fear into them, he otherwise had no other physical contact with them. He had two associates who worked with him. In exchange for the duties they performed for him, they were able to use the girls as they pleased during whatever downtime they had between clients.

It was two years before Crystal was promoted to being a house girl. By that time, she was unrecognizable as the vibrant twenty-one-year-old girl she once was. Her hair was cropped short, and her tired eyes carried the weight of what seemed to be a lot longer period of torture than the two years she had endured. Her spirit was crushed but not quenched completely. From that first day, she decided to do whatever she had to do until the opportunity to escape presented itself. She was able to endure each atrocity and the fullness of her clients' depravity only by keeping the hope of escape close to her heart. It was almost seven years later before she was able to escape.

There is no special story involving that escape. She just waited one night until she knew everyone was asleep and climbed out a first-floor window. She was ashamed to go home because she could not bear to tell her family what had happened to her. They probably had written her off as dead, and she decided that was probably better than the truth. She had been in hiding on the streets for nearly four months up until the day she walked into Thicker than Water Ministries for a meal and some air-conditioned comfort from the heat.

She was expecting the usual "steaming pot of soup, slice of bread, and can of pop" meal typical of these kinds of church outreaches. The meal was served in a dining room at one end of the ministry building. The kitchen was modern and big enough to serve large crowds of people. The staff was very kind, and she found their warmth comforting. When she arrived at the counter, she was offered a choice of fried chicken or a cheeseburger. She nearly fell over from shock, and it took her a couple minutes in her disbelief before she actually answered. After moving through the line along the counter, the meal she had on the tray before her was of genuine restaurant quality. At the end of the line, a lady at a cash register tallied up a total, and she felt for a second as if she was in the wrong place.

The lady must have read her thoughts, because she smiled and said to her, "It's okay, honey. We just have to add up how much food we give away. At the end of the evening, there is a gentleman from our church that will write a check for the entire amount. Enjoy your meal."

Crystal was touched. She made her way to the far end of the dining room and picked a seat that allowed her to see whoever came into the room. The food was amazing. As she sat in that dining room eating that wonderful meal, she almost started to feel human again. She took the time to savor each bite. Crystal estimated that there were about forty people in the room sitting and eating. Her estimates were usually pretty accurate because of all her years in the family ministry. You get to be good at figuring out how many people are in a room when you perform for crowds of various sizes.

From where she was sitting, she could see the entire dining room as well as back into the kitchen. She watched the number of people slowly dwindle into the evening until there were only five diners left. She heard laughter in the kitchen and looked up from the comfortable peace of her table to see what was happening. A man had arrived there and was working his way through greetings with all the kitchen staff. He was short, but even from where she was sitting, she could see his muscular build. His head was shaved, and his eyes were a deep shade of blue that she could also see clearly from where she was sitting. He worked his way out into the dining room and began greeting the handful of diners that remained. She noticed him looking in her direction from the time he entered the dining room but tried to tell herself it was nothing. Months of being in hiding had left her overcautious. She was in a church miles away from Julius, and there was no way he would know anyone here. As he worked his way around the room toward her, she became uneasy. She was tired of running, she was tired of where life had taken her, and all she wanted to do was find some rest.

The man walked up to her and said, "You know, there is nowhere you can hide from him."

Her heart sank. All her running and hiding had ended, and now this muscle-bound guy was here to drag her out of air-conditioned comfort and back into slavery at the hands of Julius. He was going to be so angry that she would be lucky if she survived the beating she was sure to get. All her sadness and anguish came rushing upon her in this moment, and she burst into tears. Giant, uncontrollable sobs heaved from her frail body and shook the table she was sitting at. The kitchen staff and the handful of diners all looked in her direction.

With her last bit of energy spent in this moment, she spoke through her sobs and said, "Okay, just take me to him and get it over with. I am tired of running. I cannot do this anymore. I am done running!"

A few of the ladies from the kitchen started to come out of the kitchen toward her table, but the man waved at them and signified for them to stay in the kitchen. Her mind raced as she tried to imagine what horrors would be visited upon her. She expected the guy to grab her at any second or take out a cell phone to call Julius and tell him she had been found. All the terrible things she imagined in this moment of pregnant silence seemed to hang in the air like a thick fog. At last, the man spoke and broke through that fog. His voice was gentle but somehow had strength at the same time.

"I'm sorry, sister, but I am not who you think I am. I saw you sitting here in the corner by yourself and jokingly meant that you could not hide from God where you are sitting. My name is Craig, and I am the pastor here at Thicker Than Water. I do not know whom you are hiding from or how long you have been hiding from them, but you have found safety. Let me have a lady from the kitchen come and sit here with you until we can get things locked up, and then we can sit together and talk about just how safe you are now. You have just unknowingly walked into the perfect place, and you are right…you are done running."

Pastor Craig smiled warmly at her and got up from the table. He walked over to the kitchen and spoke briefly to one of the ladies. The rest of the staff went to work closing the kitchen, but the lady Pastor Craig had spoken to walked slowly to the table and took a seat across from Crystal.

She said, "Hi, honey, my name is Sheila. Pastor Craig asked me to come and sit with you while we close things down. Do you have any personal belongings outside that we can bring in for you before we lock the doors?"

Crystal was so shocked at this turn of events that she could not speak. Pastor Craig's words echoed in her ears as if they had been spoken in a dream or played for her on some type of underwater sound device. She suddenly had so many questions that she did not know which one to ask first. Things had seemed to turn around for her so suddenly and drastically that for a moment, she had forgotten that the lady, Sheila, had asked her a question.

Somehow, while choking back what remained of her previously uncontrolled sobbing, she answered, "Nothing that matters."

After about twenty minutes, the kitchen was closed and the few remaining diners had left. The staff had shut the lights off, and Pastor Craig hugged each of them and thanked them for their hard work as they left. Each of them flashed a brief smile in her direction as they left. There was something behind those smiles, but Crystal would not learn what it was until later. Each of them waved goodbye to Sheila as they walked out the door, and Pastor Craig locked the door behind the last one. Crystal watched him go around and check all the doors to be sure they were locked, and then he came and sat down next to Sheila across the table from her. This time, she looked into his deep-blue eyes. What she found there was what she had always thought should have been in the eyes of her father...love.

He smiled warmly at her once again and said, "We are going to help you whether or not you ever tell us your story. You do not have to tell us your real name. If you have murdered someone or have done some horrible thing to a child, we will have to report you to the police. If you are in immediate danger, it would benefit you to tell us so we know whom it is we are protecting you from. The church owns a small apartment building nearby, and there is a room available there for you to stay in rent-free until you get things sorted out. Meanwhile, if you want, you can work here in the kitchen for a little cash to help you get back on your feet. We get funding from so many sources that you never have to worry about being a burden to us. We will help you, and all we ask for in return is that as soon as you are able, you work with us to help others."

With that being said, Pastor Craig and Sheila both smiled warmly at her and waited patiently to see how she would respond. At first, all she could do is ask, "Is this for real? Is this really happening?" It was just after 9:00 p.m. when Crystal asked those two questions. Both Pastor Craig and Sheila assured her that the offer was real and that her running had truly ended. Through tears and a box of tissues, Crystal told them her entire story. She left out no details. Pastor Craig asked a few questions but, for the most part, just listened intently. For some parts of the story, Sheila cried almost as much as Crystal did. It was after 1:30 a.m. when Crystal finally finished telling them her story. She felt as if a giant weight had lifted from her shoulders. She took a deep breath and waited to see what the next step was.

It was Pastor Craig who first spoke up and broke the silence. "Crystal, I know you have endured more than any normal person should ever have to endure, but you need to endure just a little more. You have a responsibility to those girls who are still in bondage by Julius's hand. I have a friend that is a detective. I need you to find the strength to work with him to find Julius and free those other girls. Can you do that?"

Crystal answered, "I ran for my life, and I have no idea where that house is. It was months ago, and it was nighttime when I took off."

He replied, "There may be some small detail about the area that meant nothing to you but might mean something to my friend. Are you willing to try?"

Crystal agreed to talk to the detective and expressed her gratitude to both Craig and Sheila. They all exchanged hugs and left for the night. Pastor Craig went home, and Sheila walked Crystal to the apartment building. Sheila offered Crystal a couch in her apartment until the next day when she could get a key for her own room. The pair stayed up until dawn talking to each other before finally retiring to bed.

As Crystal lay awake, waiting for sleep to find her, her thoughts drifted toward her family. She had lost hope for a long time. She surprisingly realized how much she missed them all. She was unsure what the coming weeks held for her, but she could already feel some hope that everything was going to work out. She fell asleep with a smile on her face and a peace in her heart that escaped any understanding.

CHAPTER 4
A Day in the Life (Part Two)

Misty slowly peeled the filthy clothing off her body and stuffed it into a trash bag. She had a fireplace in her apartment, but she was repulsed by the possibility of the smell from them filtering through her apartment. She lived a half hour away from where the job had gone bad, so she decided it would be safe to put that bag out with her usual trash in the apartment dumpster. Her mind was racing as she recollected the day's events, and she decided that a hot shower might help to clear her mind.

As the hot water cascaded over her body, washing the filth and tension away, she also took some time to clear her mind and relax her breathing. By the time she was showered and dried off, she was in a state of total peace and ready to turn her thoughts to what went wrong today. This was a perfectly planned job, and it should have gone quickly and efficiently. Not only was her mark not in the vehicle he was supposed to be in, but there were several dead cops and an unintended victim in the alley as well. This job had turned to chaos, and she had no idea yet what had happened or where the flaw in her planning was. She decided that it might be a good idea to watch some of the local news to find out what everyone else knew. She went to the kitchen and poured herself a glass of wine and then settled in her recliner in front of the television.

"In our breaking news story this evening, a failed attempt on alleged mob boss Anthony Ferranti left three police officers dead and a lot of questions unanswered for authorities. Police say that one man was rushed to the hospital and is under police guard for questioning

concerning the situation. They were unwilling to comment any further concerning who the man was or what his involvement might
have been."

Misty knew they were talking about the one called Miller. She
turned the events of the day around in her mind. Miller was already
at the door of the limo when she dropped down into it. The guards
had all been right where they were supposed to be, but Miller was a
complete surprise. There was no doubt that they knew she was coming but did not know who to look for. She dressed seductively on
purpose when men were involved because she knew that her beauty
was distracting to them. She caught the first bodyguard totally by
surprise, so that told her they did not know who they were looking for. But the fact that Miller showed up so quickly, added to the
fact that Ferranti was not in the limo, implied that they knew an
attempt on his life was going to happen. They probably had told
the guards to act natural and stick to the routine in order to not tip
off the would-be assassin that they knew what was going to happen.
She figured Miller was probably a professional Ferranti hired as a
counterassassin.

He was surprisingly agile in those blue snakeskin boots. He was
not hesitant at all with the trigger of that shotgun. She wondered
how he was going to explain why he killed the horse-mounted police
officer. A professional killer would not take the risk of killing a cop
in broad daylight. The only way that was not a factor is if Miller was
contracted by the military. If that was true, that would mean Ferranti
had protection from the military though. She had spent months
gathering intelligence for this job. The questions she now had were
disturbing to her due to the implication that she was intentionally
fed false information. It was either that, or that someone had dou-
ble-crossed her and sold her out to Ferranti. She decided that the first
thing she needed to do was find out who Miller was.

"Around noon today, an unidentified female assailant killed
five of Ferranti's bodyguards outside the entrance of the Clandestine
Hotel and two others who were posted across the street. She entered
his limousine through an open sunroof and killed the driver.
Witnesses say an additional bodyguard fired two shots into the limo,

attempting to kill the female, but somehow she escaped and fled on horseback. Police are examining various photos and amateur video witnesses took at the scene but say none of the footage so far helps to identify the woman. Mounted officer Levi Wolfe was shot and killed in the altercation between the woman and Ferranti's armed body-guard. Sources say that this bodyguard is the man that was rushed to County General Hospital, but the reports are unconfirmed."

She sipped her wine and thought about where she might have gotten wrong information from. The internet yielded a lot of infor-mation concerning who Ferranti's men were, as well as what the background was on each man. Building schematics for other build-ings in the area were easily accessed, as well as security risks pre-sented by cameras on the surrounding buildings that needed to be disabled. She had secretly taken several photos of Ferranti's men and various other hotel staff to determine the differences between the two in order to minimize collateral damage during the hit. The fact that Miller did not show up at all prior to the hit seemed to confirm that he was recently hired for this occasion. After some deeper thought, she concluded that the breakdown in her planning was centered on one thing: it was Ferranti's schedule. He was supposed to be in that limo, but he was not. This meant a trip to Ting Ting's bookstore.

She hated working with Ting and did not trust him from the beginning. His store was in Ferranti's territory, which meant he had to pay kickbacks to him. It was this fact that Misty exploited when she initially contacted Ting. No one enjoys paying protection money, and turning people against the one who collects it is usually pretty simple. Ting ran a very successful adult bookstore, and it was for this reason she despised him. It was widely whispered that he ran an escort service out of that location as well, but Misty never saw evidence of that the few times she had been there. It was the over-whelming amount of disgusting pornographic materials in the store that disgusted her. Ting was a fat, chauvinistic pig of a human being as well, and he hit on her every time she went there. He had moved here from China nearly twenty-five years ago, and it was a curious fact to her that she was unable to find any information about him prior to his moving here from there. She figured he had probably fled the country to avoid some sexually based charges, but she did not spend too much time looking into him because he was not part of the job at hand. In the moment, she decided it might not be a bad idea to look a little deeper into his past.

"Further reports indicate that shortly after fleeing the scene of the crime on Officer Wolfe's horse, Officer Pete Baker collided with the woman on horseback with his cruiser. Officer Baker only suffered minor injuries. He was treated and released on the scene, but the front end of his cruiser was demolished. The horse died on impact. The mysterious woman then fled into a nearby alley and killed a homeless man in order to steal his clothing to aid in her escape. The identity of the homeless man has not yet been released."

Misty wrestled with killing people. She was trained at a very young age, and it was all she had ever known. One of the ways she had dealt with the anxiety of her profession was that she did her best to only kill bad people. From time to time, an innocent bystander was harmed or killed, but she always did her best to minimize those kinds of situations. Killing the homeless man was a necessity in her escape, but she was slightly upset with herself for not trying to find another way. Homeless people have so little that she felt bad taking his clothing. He seemed to be asleep when she rounded that corner, and in the heat of the moment, she quickly decided that killing him would deliver him from whatever circumstances led him to where he was. Snapping his neck was quick and painless as possible and did not leave a messy wound. She wondered if he had any family to notify once he was identified. Her profession had allowed her to travel the world. She had enough money in the bank to never have to work again if she decided not to. Killing is all she had ever done, and as often as she contemplated not doing it anymore, she had no idea what else to do if she ever did quit. She had learned to convince herself that the world was somehow better off without the souls she had released from it.

"Shortly afterward, the mysterious woman was involved in a shootout with police a couple of blocks away while attempting to board a city bus. The suspect disappeared into the city sewer system shortly afterward, and the search for her continues at this hour. Police have brought in extra canine units from nearby precincts to aid in the search but do not seem to be optimistic that they will find out who this woman was or where she came from. We here at Channel Six share our condolences for the loss of those brave officers involved in this terrible situation, and our hearts go out to their families."

Of all the emotions that Misty experienced in these quiet moments, the primary one that surfaced was anger. So much senseless loss of life was the result of whomever it was that ruined the perfect planning of this job. As the news continued through weather and other items, she was consumed with finding out where the planning process broke down and killing whomever was responsible. It appeared thus far from the newscast that she had created enough confusion in her escape that she would not be identified. Every cell phone has a camera, so in a case where a job has to be done in broad daylight, she was careful to generate enough fear and confusion to cut down on the possibility of bystanders snapping clear pictures or taking video. The news came to an end, and the typical late-night programming began. Misty was lost in thought and turning the events of the day over in her mind. She was swiftly brought out of her contemplation by another breaking news story. It was approaching two in the morning, and she wondered what event could be so pressing as to become breaking news at this late hour. The report continued.

"Preliminary investigations have identified the homeless victim of today's assault at the Clandestine Hotel. Police believe the victim to be Roland Scott. Scott is the primary suspect in a series of serial killings reaching back nearly ten years. This is an unprecedented situation that adds even more questions to an already troubling and mysterious series of events. When questioned, a source in police headquarters would not speculate concerning whether or not they believe Scott's murder was related to the events at the Clandestine or just a coincidence. We will continue to keep you informed as authorities sort out the details in this bizarre chain of events."

Misty was speechless.

What were the odds in the chaos of this horribly failed job that the random victim she killed in an alley would wind up being a serial killer who had avoided capture by the police for nearly ten years? She had been wrestling with a small amount of guilt for taking his life all evening. Suddenly, her thoughts spun out of control in an entirely different direction. Killing the man in the alley was a spur-of-the-moment decision. Would she have acted differently knowing who the man was? She never took pleasure in killing. She turned herself off emotionally whenever she had to do it. Over time, she had learned to compartmentalize that part of what she did and detach herself from it. She lied to herself while she was investigating and planning and made it into a kind of game. When all the pieces were in place, she "switched off" and took whatever lives were needed by the job. She did not consider motive or reason. She never asked herself whether or not the victims deserved to die. Those kinds of questions cloud your judgment and keep you from doing the job effectively.

The problem with this situation was that for the first time, Misty wrestled with the idea that this person probably deserved to die. If it actually turned out that the man she killed at random in the alley was secretly a serial killer, then she was actually glad he was dead. The conflicting thought was that she had probably taken many more lives than he ever did, so did that make her even more deserving of death in someone else's eyes? Was she really any better than him? In a basic sense, she created grief, loss, and even sometimes suffering the same as he had. How was she any different from him?

CHAPTER 5
Ting Ting's Bookstore

Chinatown…

It is midevening, and the shadows are growing longer in the streets as day turns to night. Merchants are busy carrying their product indoors from the sidewalks. Earlier in the day, you could hardly press your way through the consumers, and the pickpockets, but the street is nearly empty of people now. You could sum up the entire scene unfolding before you with two words: "closing time."

Barely noticeable among the cluster of so many shops in this small area, one discreet sign in a caged window reads "Adult Books." A small stairway leads to the thick wooden door that opens into the bookstore. The store is dimly lit and seems overstocked with adult oriented materials. The observant person would notice that, beyond the distraction provided by all the merchandise, the interior of the store is in a sad state of disrepair. The paint is peeling from the walls as if they were shedding a layer of off-white skin in giant blistering sores. In one of the corners, the ceiling tiles are slowly rotting away and falling into a heap of damp, moldy asbestos on the floor. The shop itself has an old musty-type smell that hangs loosely in the air like a mildew ghost. Despite these conditions, the merchandise is new, and all the current adult films are in stock.

The shop owner is a Chinese man named Ting Ting. He is an older man in his late fifties. He has some gray hairs peeking through the black hair, which he combs sloppily over his growing bald spot. He is fat and out of shape, and he has to stop and catch his breath after the least amount of physical exertion. He has a cataract in one eye that leaves it milky white and adds to the overall Mole Man look he seems to have. He is standing behind the register, counting the money he has made today, when he hears a soft female voice behind him say (in Chinese), "Okay, you fat sack of flesh! Tell me a story about missing marks and security guards that wear expensive blue snakeskin boots. If I like the story, you can keep counting the money. If I don't…well, let's just say that this is not a toothpick."

That being said, he notices something sharp poking him at the base of his neck. He does not even have to turn around to know who this stranger is that snuck up behind him in the shadows. He masks the fear swelling in his heart as he starts to wonder what hideous instrument of torture might be pointed at his neck if he has guessed rightly. In a fearful and trembling voice, he manages to say (also in Chinese), "Misty, is that you?"

With serious anger and a touch of sarcasm in her voice, she says softly, "Ever hear of the tooth fairy? Well, I am the head fairy, and if you don't start talking soon, there is going to be about ten pounds of ugly under your pillow tonight."

There is now no doubt in Ting Ting's mind who it is behind him. He looks around on the counter in front of him for anything he can use as a weapon. He is nervous, and in just the few seconds he has been in this position, he is already dripping with sweat. He realizes that if he does not say something soon, the opportunity to say anything will be gone. He knows Misty is serious. He knows that she is angry. Most of all, he knows that if she finds out the truth of what he has been doing lately, she will hurt him—badly.

The seconds are ticking away fast, and he knows he has to do something quickly, or else, death is imminent. In those last few seconds before whatever is poking in his neck can be driven home, he says a name. "Xiao Zhou."

There are a few seconds of complete silence. Silence, in fact, is an understatement. It is as if a black hole has suddenly materialized in the center of the room and has started sucking every ounce of air out of the little shop. For that span of seconds, Ting Ting wonders if he has said the right or wrong thing. For those few seconds, he will never know how close he came to a very bloody and painful demise.

Clearly upset, Misty finally manages to ask another question. "TT, why are you lying to me? If *he* had anything to do with this, *you* just mentioning his name would mean certain death!" Some of the confidence has drained from her voice though, because it makes sense to her that Ting Ting's boss would not take kindly to the fact that his subordinate was being forced to pay the local mob boss a fee for protection. He would definitely order the hit on Ferranti, but this still leaves a mystery concerning who alerted the mob boss that a hit was coming.

Ting Ting knows he has said enough to delay his execution. He straightens himself, and in a relaxed voice, he says, "Or else certain death to *you*, baby, if you kill me and deny *him* the opportunity."

She is frustrated now, because she wants to cancel this fat pig of a man out and leave his body to the flies, but she knows she cannot. Killing this underling will draw unwanted attention from his boss that she really doesn't need at the moment. She slowly pulls the fountain pen that she had pressed against his neck away and sets it on the counter in front of him. He wipes the sweat from his forehead and looks down at the pen with distaste in his eyes.

"That is my favorite pen," he says.

"Yeah, mine too. I was thinking about writing my name on your brainstem with it," she replies. She backs away from him a few steps in order to allow him some room to turn around. She also decides that his smell is sickening to her, and she needs a little distance.

He turns and looks her briefly in the eyes. Then, he slowly looks her up and down from head to toe. As he is drinking her in inch by inch, his mind fills with a myriad of sexual images, and his eyes move slowly up her body. Those thoughts are immediately squashed as he locks eyes with her once again and sees the murderous anger in her eyes that he missed the first time. He finds enough courage for one more wisecrack. "Yes, but then you couldn't make love to me, and I *know* you want to."

With a speed that can only be described as supernatural, she has the pen in her hand once again. Before his reflexes can even react, the point of the pen is no less than a millimeter away from the center of his left eyeball. For a split second, he is sure that his last comment was too much and now he is going to die. He follows the point of the pen up her arm and looks her in the eyes. What he sees is the most horrifying thing yet since this encounter began—what he will remember most about this brief meeting with the woman the underworld knows as Razormist: her devious smile.

"Ting Ting, if anyone asks you if you've seen me, tell them you are keeping an eye out for me, okay...baby?" and with that, she stabs the pen deep into his eye socket. She is just about to make her grand exit when suddenly she hears the slight jingle from the bells that hang by the door that enters the shop from the street. TT is screaming at the top of his lungs from the eye socket wound, so whoever has just walked in knows instantly that something is wrong. She decides that the element of surprise is her best defense, so she leaps the counter and starts in the direction of the front door.

"Hey yo, TT, is that you? Where you at you potbellied pig?"

His name is Joey Arbuckle. He works for the local mob boss, Ferranti, and he is here to collect his weekly payment for the mob's protection. He has thick black hair that is pulled back into a tight ponytail. He is a large kid and has a muscular build. Joe has worked for the mob some time now and has some street toughness about him. He attends a local gym in the area and held a Golden Gloves boxing title for three years straight when he was slightly younger. He rounds the corner of some shelves and sees Ting Ting bent over the counter. TT is screaming and covering his left eye with both hands. There is blood everywhere.

"TT, what happened? Who done this to you?"

Years of being a street thug has built an almost sixth sense in times of trouble for Joe. He instantly turns to look around and see if whoever has bloodied TT is still nearby. He no sooner starts this looking when, out of the shadows, he sees a figure coming at him full force. His reflexes are good, and despite how fast the blow was coming at him, he is somehow able to deflect it. It would have been a solid punch to his jawline, a punch Joe would refer to as a "sleeper." Almost simultaneously, Joe thinks about the deadly force of the punch he has just dodged and catches a knee right in his chest. The breath goes out of him in a painful rush. In the midst of this savage attack, Joe is mystified as he catches a glance of who it is he has been jumped by. She is *gorgeous!* She is clearly Asian, and she clearly means business. He dodges another punch and lifts his knee to block the knee she throws at his chest the second time. He lurches forward in that instant and pushes her a few feet away. "I don't know who you are, whore, but you gonna be *real* sorry for that!"

She watches his weight shift. This big oaf has underestimated her, and she can tell by the look in his eyes that he is blinded by rage. She sees his muscles tense and prepares for the blow that she knows is about to come. For a second, she says to herself, *He's really going to jump at me. Sloppy fighter. He has no concept of who he's dealing with. I guess I will have to teach him!*

"See how you like this!" Joe says as he leaps in her direction.

At just the right moment, while Joe's momentum is carrying him toward her, she launches into a backflip. She whips her back foot into the flip and catches Joe right under the chin with it while still in midair. The force of the kick is devastating and sends Joe backward with such force that he shatters the glass on the front of the display counter a full five feet behind him. As soon as her feet touch the floor, she is instantly in motion toward Joe. She stops short and plants her right foot firmly against his throat.

"Don't bother getting up, big boy. I was just leaving," she says, and then she adds, "And, TT, you keep an eye out for me, sweetie."

With that, she merely turns and walks toward the door. She is amused by the moaning and shouting of the two men behind her as she goes. She gives no thought that either of them might try to get her as she exits the store. The agonizing sounds of pain and mutilation coming from behind her are proof enough that all the fight is gone from them. As she walks through the door, there is an older man on the walk who appears to be preparing to enter the store.

"I think they are closed. Come back tomorrow," she says to the man, extending a slightly distasteful smile in his direction. The man looks upset for just a moment but appears to take her at her word as he turns and heads away from the store.

As she walks away from the store and down the street, she is clearly troubled at what she has just heard. She still walks with an almost feline grace, so much so that it is as if she is floating instead of walking. Her long black ponytail swings gently back and forth with each step that she takes. To the whole outside world, Misty is just a gorgeous Asian female out for an evening stroll. In fact, the only way you could tell that she is troubled is if you were able to look deep into her mysterious green eyes.

Back at Ting Ting's bookstore, two men are slowly recovering from their recently acquired wounds. Joe was the first to regain his composure. He stood to his feet and managed to shake the loose glass off his clothing. He was thankful to find that none of the shards of glass had pierced his new leather jacket. He went into the back room of the store to get some paper towels for the bloody mess from TT's eye socket wound. By this time, Ting Ting apparently figured out that all the screaming in the world would not ease the pain now emanating in nauseating waves from his left eye socket. He has moved now to shouting obscenities describing the various sexual violations he would like to commit against Misty for what she has done. This wave of filthy verbal corruption could only be spawned from the lips of an old man who has spent his life peddling every kind of pornography known to man. The things he shouts are *so* vile and vulgar that to hear them would be so shocking as to inspire a fit of hysterical laughter—as if such violations were humanly possible.

CHAPTER 6
A Change of Fortune

Everything changed the day the bad news came.

Paul was attracted to Julianna from the start. He knew she was way out of his league but could not help but think about her. Two encounters with her had been burned into his mind since they attended middle school together. When the bad news first came, he first remembered these two encounters.

He had always admired her beauty from afar and never dared approach her. She was tall and had long beautiful brown hair. Her body was slender, and she walked with an athletic grace that seemed more like gliding than walking at the time. She had fine facial features that caused her whole face to light up when she smiled. Of all the things to admire about her, it was the piercing blue-green eyes haunted him night and day. He could not look into those eyes for more than a few seconds without becoming breathless, fearful, and at the same time, energized. He endured the daily torment, bullying, and schoolwork because each day brought with it the chance to steal a glance at Julianna. Even now, as an adult, she was the golden standard by which he judged the attractiveness of every other female he encountered. They had been married for five years when the news came, and he still lost his breath slightly when he looked into those eyes.

The first encounter happened one day in the lunch line. He had gotten in line without noticing she was in front of him, and other kids began forming the line behind him. He was paralyzed, hoping she would not turn around and look at him with those eyes. One of the meaner kids in line right behind him hit his hand and caused it to bump her right on her rear end. He was immediately terrified, and what seemed like an electric shock of horror passed through him. She turned around, smiled weakly at him, and turned her attention back toward whatever was in front of her. He could have died right there in that line. This was the only physical contact he had with her until he had met her again all those years later, but it burned in his mind as a life-changing moment. He touched her, and she did not disappear like a soap bubble popping in the summer air. She was real, and he swore he could, days after it happened, still feel the exact spot on his hand that touched her.

The second encounter happened during the following summer of that same school year. He was riding bikes with one of his friends, and his friend mentioned that he knew right where she lived. This fact rolled from his friend's mouth so matter-of-factly, as if it was passing knowledge shared by everyone. When his friend mentioned stopping by to say hi to her, it was all he could do to restrain himself. Even now, he can remember every small detail of that house and that agonizingly slow walk up the driveway of Julianna's house. The driveway ran alongside the right side of the house and up into a small carport. The house was a dark maroon color, and even though it was daytime, the carport shrouded the door to the house in shadow. It was a very brief visit. She stepped out the back door and said hi to them. He remembered wanting to stay there and talk forever, but his friend cut the visit short by saying they just wanted to drop by and say hi. Her eyes locked with his for that brief moment, and for years, he wondered if he should have asked her out. Should he have taken the shot? He did not see her again for years after that. All he knew was that when they returned to school that next year, she was gone. He did not dare ask any of his classmates for fear of the ridicule he might face for letting his feelings for her be known.

He had always been the awkward kid in school. His clothing was awkward, he had bad acne, and in a generation of kids consumed by television and other distractions, very few of them could relate to his taste for reading books. He was never really the athletic type and had no interest in sports. He had very few friends back then, and those school years did not carry the fondest of memories for him. He was happy when he graduated high school and put all that behind him.

He held several small jobs after graduation, but nothing really caught on and held his interest. He was still living at home in his parents' house at twenty years old and had not yet found any purpose or direction for his life. Each day faded into the next until life became a blur of years, with nothing of any significance attached to it. Paul was a daydreamer. The life he imagined for himself was entirely different from the automated routine that his true life reflected. He desperately wanted to travel the world. He wanted to get away from his life, so he was always more focused on where he wanted to go than where he currently was. He was not reckless with money, but his career choices did not provide him with the finances to build the life he had constructed in his mind. His first purchase out of high school was a new two-seater sports car. He never missed a payment, but with the insurance payments as they were for a boy right out of high school, there was little else he could afford. His change of fortune began at twenty years old, while he was working at a company that sold battery-operated toys. It was when he first met Craig.

Craig was an intense person, and he had an energy about him like no one else Paul had ever met. Sometimes you meet a person and automatically like them for some reason as soon as you meet them. This was the case with Craig, and something about him was just contagious. Craig and Paul worked together in the warehouse of the company and split the shipping and receiving tasks between themselves. What Paul appreciated most about Craig was that although they worked together in the same place, Craig was sure this was a stop for him toward bigger things. Craig had a sense of some larger purpose to his life that he had not yet found. He was a revolutionary, and Paul had no doubt even then that Craig was destined for some kind of greatness. He convinced Paul that no matter how ridiculous they might seem now, his daydreams might actually be part of his purpose in life. They worked well together and even spent some time hanging out with each other outside of work. Craig was his first good friend, but he had no idea at the time how significant that friendship would become.

Paul's birthday was in February, and he had started working at the toy company with Craig the first week of March after his twentieth birthday. In October of that same year, both of Paul's parents were killed in a horrible car accident. Paul was devastated. He was totally unprepared for an event of this magnitude. His parents were loving people, and he was immediately ashamed for having not taken the time to communicate his appreciation to them for that. They faithfully attended church every Sunday, and he had never gone with them one time even though they had invited him repeatedly. Despite that, it was the church people who embraced him most of all and helped him through the worst tragedy he had ever known. The funeral was a great tribute to the people his parents were, and he was truly touched by the love that was made evident by their church family through the process. He decided shortly after the funeral that there was nothing to tie him to his boyhood home, so he started work toward emptying and selling it. He quit his job immediately and said goodbye to Craig, intending to do what traveling he could with the money from selling the home. He was sure to get contact information from Craig, with the intention of looking him up when he returned from his travels.

Just after the house sold and while Paul was packing to leave on his journey, a man knocked on the door. His name was Bill, and he recognized him as one of the members of the church his mom and dad had attended. Paul had vaguely heard over the past few weeks that he was retired from the military and that now he was some kind of financial planner for the people of the church and their families.

Bill looked him over as he entered the house. Paul noticed a strange look about Bill like there was something he came to say, and he was busting to say it. The hidden urgency in Bill's eyes at this point was unexplainable.

Bill said, "Son, I think you might want to sit down for this one."

Paul turned over a couple heavy plastic crates he had not yet loaded. He sat on one and motioned for Bill to sit down on the other one.

Bill took the seat and immediately began with the news he had had come to deliver. "Paul, I don't know if you knew this or not, but I do some financial planning for people at the church. I have been doing this for a long time, and experience has taught me that it is best to deliver this particular kind of news to a person after having them sit down."

Paul nodded his head to verify he knew this information about Bill and in concession to the previous statement concerning his needing to be seated.

Bill continued, "Son, your parents came to me when you were first born and asked me to set up a life insurance policy so that if anything ever happened to them, you would be provided for. You have to understand that they paid into this plan your whole life. I helped them switch some of the money around and invest some of it as well over the years. You were eligible for the money on your eighteenth birthday, but your parents held back from telling you because they were waiting for the right situation in your life to surprise you with it. They were very proud of the young man you turned out to be, and the only regret they had was that they were unable to pass on a spiritual legacy to you…but besides that, you were the greatest blessing to them."

Paul looked around the house they had left behind. It was a modest home and sold for under a hundred thousand considering the size and location. He did not figure the amount of money Bill had come to present to him would be very much. He was completely unprepared then for the change of fortune about to be presented to him.

Bill pulled the check from his inside jacket pocket, and as he handed the check to him, he said, "A sum of money this substantial usually comes as a surprise to people, and the initial shock can sometimes be overwhelming at first."

Paul took the check from Bill. When he read the amount it was written for, it stole the breath from his lungs. He stared at the check in wide-eyed fascination for a few brief moments, overcome with disbelief.

Bill finally broke the silence by saying, "Well, say something, son."

"Fifty *million* dollars?" Paul finally squeezed out. "Am I reading this correctly? Fifty *million* dollars?"

Bill produced a huge smile and said, "Yes, son, you *are* reading it right. Congratulations, you are a millionaire."

It was literally about twenty minutes before Paul was able to calm down enough for any rational conversation with Bill. He shouted and jumped around the house. He screamed, and tears ran down his face in great wet streams. He shouted "THANK YOU" up at the heavens a hundred times. He hugged Bill repeatedly in all this and thanked him as well. He would regain his composure for a few moments, but then he would think again about this change of fortune and start the whole dance over again. Paul finally sat back down on the upturned crate and calmed himself down.

He turned to Bill and asked, "Is there some taxes I have to pay? Do I need to hire an accountant? Do I just take this check to the bank and make a deposit? What do I do, Bill?"

Bill smiled and answered, "Your parents tell me you are pretty wise with your money. I am sure they wanted you to enjoy it. You can take the check to your bank and deposit it. Then I suggest you go take this trip and enjoy yourself. You are not obligated to deal with me personally any more concerning this money, but if you want, you are welcome to look me up when you get back. I can help you invest the money and do some planning for the future." He handed Paul one of his business cards and stood up to leave.

Paul hugged him tightly and said, "Bill, I would not *dream* of trusting anyone but you to help me with this. My parents trusted you, and it worked out well for them. I *promise* I will look you up as soon as I get back. Thank you *so much* for doing this for me and my parents." Bill smiled at him, nodded his head, and with a few more words of encouragement to have a great time, he was gone. Paul finished packing the few things he had. He stopped at the bank and deposited the check in his account. He purchased a small storage unit and paid for ten years in advance with the agreement that he would settle up for the balance either way when he returned from his trip.

In all this, he had decided there was one more thing he wanted to do. It required a couple more stops, but in his mind, it was worth it.

When Craig walked out at the end of his shift that day, he was surprised to see Paul standing there in the parking lot. Paul was grinning from ear to ear and waved at him when he noticed him walking out to his car. Craig listened in disbelief as Paul relayed the day's events to him. When the story was over, there was one last question hanging unanswered. "So what are you doing here then?" Craig asked.

Paul answered, "You have been my best friend, man, and I thought about this today. I need a ride to the airport. If you don't mind, and it doesn't offend you, I want to give my car to you. I already stopped and paid it off. We can stop at the BMV on the way to the airport and sign it over to your name. The title is in the glove box. It is only two years old, and you *know* I have taken care of it. I will not need it where I am going, and I will probably just buy a new one whenever I come back. I know you and your wife need a second car, and I would feel better knowing I gave my baby to someone who will take care of her."

Craig could not believe his ears, but after a few moments, he hugged Paul and said, "Get in, I'm driving!" Craig placed a quick call to his wife with his cell phone to tell her he would be late getting home and said he would explain later. She heard he was with Paul and said to tell him hello and then got off the phone. Craig took ownership of the car and then drove Paul to the airport. He walked with his friend to the gate and waited with him until he boarded the plane. As Paul was walking away to board his plane, Craig said to him, "Be *sure* and find me when you come back! I will want to hear about your travels…and thanks again for that car! I will run it to death and blow it up I promise!" He said this last part with a huge smile.

Paul replied, "Okay, just don't kill yourself in the process." In a moment, he was gone. This was the last time he saw Craig for many years. He never forgot his best friend. He thought of him every once in a while. It was nearly ten years before he returned to his hometown. After all that time, Craig had faded from his memory, and he had lost track of him. The contact information he had kept was outdated, but he was determined to look him up once his financial responsibilities were settled. He would never have guessed the means by which he and his friend would be reunited.

He rented an apartment near downtown and retrieved his things from storage right after he came back. He had contacted Bill a couple weeks in advance and made an appointment to meet him a couple days after his return. There was a nice little coffee shop across the street from his apartment building. He had called Bill and suggested they meet in that coffee shop because he had just returned and had not bought a new car yet. He had kept in contact with Bill from time to time during his travels to make investments, and he was excited to see him again now that he had made it home. He paid Bill a handsome amount of money while he was gone and trusted him a great deal. Bill had made enough from being Paul's financial adviser to open a nice office for himself downtown, as well as build a lucrative business in financial planning. Over the years, Bill had become a father figure to Paul, and this meeting was more like a family reunion for both of them rather than a business meeting. Paul arrived first and found a seat for himself as the standing sign inside the door indicated. Each time a person entered the coffee shop, Paul found himself looking expectantly at the door looking to see if it was Bill.

When Bill entered, Paul stood, and they hugged each other tightly. Paul motioned for Bill to take the seat in the small booth opposite him, and then sat down himself.

Paul said, "You look great, old friend. All that money hasn't changed you one bit."

Bill laughed and answered, "Well, my suits are a little nicer, but you wouldn't know a thing about that, son."

Bill was right. Paul never owned a suit, and formal wear for him was a button-up dress shirt with his jeans. The two began immediately swapping stories and catching up with each other. They were laughing and chatting for about fifteen minutes when the waitress finally came and asked them if they were ready to order. Bill looked the menu over briefly, and Paul just slid the menu over to her and ordered a Diet Mountain Dew. When he looked up and made eye contact with the waitress, her blue-green eyes caught his attention. At first, her eyes seemed familiar to him, but in the moment, he could not place from where. Then like a shovelful of wet snow hitting him in the face, he realized who she was...

It was Julianna...the waitress was Julianna.

There has never been a more pregnant moment of silence. Bill saw the reaction on Paul's face but had no idea what had taken place. He defined it as "love at first sight," but could not have understood how overwhelmed Paul was at finding himself face-to-face with his middle school crush. After all these years, Paul had never forgotten Julianna. Every female he had ever seen was measured against the image he held in his mind of her. She had what seemed to be heaviness to her spirit that most likely found its source in the trials that life had dealt to her. Paul noted that her features had not changed though, and she still looked young and vibrant. This was much more than love at first sight for Paul. The unexpectedness of the moment erased all those years of experience and traveling and turned him at once back into that awkward middle school boy struck speechless in the presence of such beauty.

Julianna recognized Paul right away but had to think for a moment to remember his name. She noted a rugged handsomeness had been added to his once boyish features. She had no idea who the older man was sitting with him, but his reaction to Paul's seemingly stunned silence in the moment caught her attention. She, of course, had no idea how Paul felt about her. She had no idea that he carried an image in his mind of her through all these years. She could not have understood in this moment the fear and wonder swelling inside Paul right here at this table, so it was Julianna who finally spoke up and broke the silence. The pregnancy of this moment gave birth to so many things with the utterance of only nine words: "Hi, Paul, how have you been all these years?"

Paul was slightly shocked that she recognized him. He had always imagined her living some extravagant life in Paris as a super-model or jetting around the world and posing for magazine covers. She was beautiful and intelligent, and he wondered what twists and turns occurred in her life that brought her to waitressing as a career choice. Somehow in the storm of thoughts and emotions her appearance stirred within him, he found his way back to the reason he was sitting at the table in the first place. He had become a world traveler, a rich international businessman, and had acquired a great deal of wisdom and strength in the process. Julianna was not wearing a wedding ring, and the fact that she was waitressing might imply that some calamity had befallen her in a past relationship, causing her to have to start over. He realized that this in fact might be an unprecedented chance to take the shot he had always wished he had taken back in middle school. The silence had just begun to turn awkward as he got himself together and finally responded to her greeting.

"Julianna, my parents died about nine years ago and left me a fortune. I just came home two days ago from traveling all over the world."

He nodded toward Bill and said, "This is my good friend and adviser, Bill." Bill and Julianna nodded at each other in recognition of the introduction.

Paul could not decipher what the look was that registered on her face in response to his reply, but now it was her turn to stand in stunned silence and prepare a reply.

"Wow, Paul, I bet you have some great stories to tell. You have come a long way since middle school."

With this reply, she unknowingly opened the door for him to take the shot he had so long waited for. He grinned, nodded slightly in Bill's direction, and said, "Bill is sick to death of my stories by now, and it would be sweet to talk to someone different who is actually interested in hearing them. would You like to meet me for dinner later?"

Once again, there was a prolonged silence hanging impossibly in the air. Paul was amazed at how simply the request had rolled from his tongue and was suddenly overcome with fear that he had blown it. He immediately second guessed himself and started going over what he had said wondering if he should have taken a more conservative approach.

Julianna slowly smiled at both men and replied, "I would love that, Paul. I get off at around seven. I will write my address down for you before you leave, and you can pick me up around seven thirty?"

Paul could not believe his ears. There was no way he actually just scored a date with the woman of his dreams. He did not want to seem overly excited, so he kept calm and agreed to what she had suggested. With that, she walked away to go put their order in.

By now, Bill was bursting with questions concerning the exchange he had just witnessed. He could hardly contain himself while he gave his order and then waited for Julianna to walk far enough from the table to be out of earshot. He knew Paul to be a hard and decisive person, and watching him practically turn into jelly in the presence of this female was very amusing. "*What* was *that* all about?" Bill asked.

Paul decided it would take too long to explain what had just transpired, so he promised to explore the topic with him after the date took place so he could add those details into what was already going to be an epic story. All at once Paul became acutely aware of how much his life had changed. He wanted for nothing, and over the past year, he had begun pondering how he might find ways to spread that good fortune to others. Julianna brought their order to the table and, along with it, a piece of paper with her contact information printed on it.

As the meal was coming to a close, Bill had one last thing he wanted to mention. "I have a guy I want to introduce to you, a client of mine. You mentioned a couple times about wanting to find a charity or program to support once you returned back to the states. I know you will like this guy, and he has some pretty radical ideas about this ministry he wants to start. I think you two will hit it off."

"Sure," Paul said. "Set up a meeting for some time late next week and let me know."

"This guy is really informal and will probably invite us to dinner at his house," Bill added.

This was interesting to Paul, but his focus was on the date he had to plan for this evening, so he quickly affirmed his decision to meet with Bill's client and brought the meeting to a close.

*****

As Paul sat back at his desk, a smile fell across his face. So much had happened in the last fifteen years that he could hardly take it all in. He had everything he could ever want. He married the girl of his dreams, but everything seemed to have lost its luster when the bad news came.

Julianna had stage 4 cancer. It was untreatable, and she was going to die.

CHAPTER 7
An Unlikely Source of Light
(Part One)

When you have to take the hard way, the path behind you is what pushes you forward.

From a very early age, Craig had a sense of some greater purpose for his life. It was something he couldn't really put his finger on, but it was always there. His mind was always alive with possibilities and ideas, and he made several attempts to make an impact on the world around him in a significant way. These, of course, never brought anything for him but doubt and frustration. It was the worst thing for Craig to carry such a burden toward greatness and yet be faced daily with the ordinary and mundane. Pain and change were a constant for him, and he lost his way several times before he found the true path.

In elementary school, Craig was always the outsider. He was awkward, distant, and had no desire to squeeze into the roles public school began to press children into. He was not interested in learning what was being taught to him and preferred to engage in his own intellectual pursuits. This meant he was not grouped with the academic achievers among his peers. He was not naturally gifted as an athlete and had a real distaste for the character he witnessed in the kids that did. This was a double-edged sword for him. He was not the strongest or fastest of his peers, which made him a target for constant bullying. That bullying, and the accompanying frustration that came with it, became the seed for a deep-seated anger that he still carried within himself to this day. These years were the most difficult for him because he had no one to turn to. He lacked the words to explain the sense of purpose tugging at his heart. None of his peers were able to think past the immediate gratification afforded to children of that age. It was a lonely time for Craig, and that loneliness did nothing but feed the helplessness, frustration, and anger that were already festering inside him.

One day, in the fifth grade, his teacher had slapped him in the face. For whatever reason, this particular teacher had developed issues with him. She had placed his desk all the way to the front of the classroom away from the other children. She propped her wooden paddle on the chalk tray right in front of his desk in an attempt to "motivate" him into completing his work. The best readers in the class met at a set of chairs just to the left of his desk for group with the teacher. Craig noticed that the stories they read and discussed were better than the ones his group worked on, so he would listen and participate with this group silently within himself. They were playing a game this day with the vocabulary words. The teacher would name one of the vocabulary words, and then the kids would name other words with the same meaning. The word "flag" was presented by the teacher, and none of the other kids could come up with a word with the same meaning. Craig almost immediately thought of the word "banner," and it struck him funny that not even the teacher could think of it. The "best" readers in the class, and even the teacher struggled with this for several moments. Craig chuckled lightly and said "Banner." The other kids were relieved that the answer was given, but apparently the teacher was unhappy about being outdone by this student she obviously did not care for.

Later that same day, he had accidently dropped his pencil on the floor. It had rolled a few feet away from his desk. For whatever reason, he saw where it dropped but got lost in a daydream and was hesitant picking it up. Craig pondered this moment every once in a while still today to try and remember where his thoughts were lost in that moment, but he could not. The teacher walked over to him, slapped him solidly on his left cheek and shouted, "Pick up that pencil and get to work!" In his mind, he grabbed that pencil, jumped on that teacher, and stabbed her repeatedly with it. His face stung the better part of the afternoon, but he was determined to not give her the satisfaction of seeing his tears. His mother visited the school the next day, and the teacher was suspended as a result. Although there were no more confrontations between him and that teacher, the damage created in him psychologically was complete. From that day forward, a seed of total disrespect toward all authority had been planted. Worse than that, this marked the first time he found comfort in fantasizing an act of violence to deal with a physical confrontation he was otherwise powerless to stop. The bullying continued, but now, so did continual thoughts of violent murder toward those peers who did the bullying. The retreats to this realm of fantasy spread into other areas of Craig's life where he felt powerless or out of control.

In middle school, the kids had for the most part been firmly pressed into the typical social cliques that naturally developed. By that time, Craig had also been firmly stuck in the role of awkward outsider. This was a constant source of inner conflict for Craig when contrasted against this inner sense of some greater purpose he still carried within himself. The reality of his life, when measured against how he felt things should be, assured that he spent more of his time fantasizing. The less like his fantasies real life became, the more his anger and frustration boiled within him.

Typically, kids become more sexually aware in middle school, and many of his peers began to pair off as boyfriend and girlfriend. Of course, none of the girls at school showed any interest in him, especially the ones he had developed crushes on. Young people are notoriously cruel with each other, and Craig was constantly jeered at and antagonized. To further complicate these issues, it was around this time that he found some old pornographic magazines his dad had brought home from his time in the Army. They were stuffed in an old Army bag in the bottom of a dusty old cabinet in the back of the garage. He had an Army hat stolen from him around that time, so his thought was that there might be an old one in with that Army stuff. Now his mind was infected at a young age with pornographic imagery to feed into his already vivid fantasy life. During the day at school, he would secretly memorize facial and body details of the girls around him as fuel for his fantasies at home each night. By the time he finished middle school, he was completely unaware of the fact that he spent more time and focus on his fantasies than he did the reality in front of him. He was socially awkward, and he was just barely passing through school by the least effort possible. His parents noticed his withdrawal and tried counseling and medication, but ultimately all they could do was watch his downward spiral.

A few unprecedented events took place during his time in high school. He found his first girlfriend during his freshman year. He had his first sexual encounter with her, which was fumbling, awkward, and nothing like what he had experienced through pornography. They were together for nearly three months before he caught her having sex with his best friend at the time. He loved her at whatever level a young high school kid can, but she made it clear to him that the relationship meant nothing to her. This affected him at a deeper level than he had ever been touched before. He decided in that moment that all females were whores to be used and discarded. He kept everyone at a distance and decided there was no one that could be trusted.

Getting his driver's license was another significant event. Driving allowed him to get away from his peers and explore other settings and groups of peers that knew nothing about him. This might have been good for him, but he used it as an opportunity to reinvent himself as the person he fantasized himself to be instead of who he truly was. He started experimenting with drugs and alcohol at that time as well. By the tenth grade, he was fully addicted to drugs and alcohol. He had friends though, and the drug culture provided a level of social interaction for him he had previously never experienced. The saying that defined that subculture was, "A friend with weed is a friend indeed." He was actually invited to parties now that his former group of peers never considered him for. He found plenty of females willing to open themselves to him. He won his first fight in his junior year. He knocked out a bully in the gym and left him twitching on the floor. It was a lucky punch, but it had a lasting effect on him. He started running, riding his bike, and lifting weights. He grew stronger for the sole purpose of inflicting pain on others—and he inflicted much pain.

He discovered that selling drugs was much more lucrative than working a minimum wage job. He worked a small number of hours as a cover for the huge amounts of money he began making from selling pot. He pulled from several different social groups so when other dealers from each group were dry and had none to sell, Craig was always holding. When he finally dropped out of high school, he had fully become the monster he had always fantasized being. He felt as if he had finally arrived. He loved his life, he felt invincible, and life was like that for a long time. There was one more event of significance toward the end of his time in high school.

He was dating a girl named Georgia. She had a rough upbringing and came from a broken home. She had made a couple attempts at suicide and spent a lot of time during their relationship in treatment centers. He cared about her, but eventually it was aggravating to him that he could not see her as often as he wanted because of the restrictions that came from being in and out of those centers. He would visit her on Friday evenings at the center she was in when the relationship ended. He would get a call more often than not from her on Wednesday that she had done something to lose her Friday evening visitation privileges. One Wednesday evening, she called him in tears about nightmares she had been having. They centered on another guy that was locked up with her in the same unit. She claimed they were vivid nightmares of him trying to kill her. This same guy that very day had approached her in the recreation yard and told her flatly that he was demonically possessed and said he was going to kill her in her sleep. He promised her he would take care of it and made her promise to not lose her visitation privileges for the approaching Friday evening. He had a small group of friends that claimed to be devil worshippers, and it was these friends he turned to for a solution.

He was intrigued by the possibility of supernatural power. He cared about Georgia, but more importantly, he craved confrontation and a chance to dominate over this guy. This end was met by a surprisingly simple ritual by which Craig became demonically possessed. He was very specific about the outcome he expected from this ritual. He said to his friends prior to the ritual, "I want whatever is inside of me to be so powerful and menacing that whatever is inside of him has no choice but to cower in fear of it." As it turned out, the guy freaked out on the Thursday night before Craig's visit and was transported to the emergency room for special care. Georgia told him that his screams could be heard all over the complex while they were hauling him out into the ambulance. He never told Georgia about the ritual or the demonic possession, and the relationship ended just a couple months later. Craig would tell you that in retrospect, the ritual was the worst decision he had ever made in his entire life. He would say, "Write the phrase 'ten years' on a piece of paper, crumple it up, and throw it away. That is the best way to describe the effect this decision had on my life." His life became a blur of drugs, sex, fighting, drunkenness, and acts of violence and open cruelty to anyone he could extend them to. He reveled in this life, but he carried a secret with him through it all. Somehow, although dimmed and choked out, that sense of purpose still nagged at him.

Long into the years of his early adulthood, Craig continued to mix his social time in different groups. In the drug culture, there is an unspoken bond that ties all people together. There were always parties to go to, people to meet, and plenty of laughter and good times. He had no idea that this crossing over between different social groups, and bringing people together over those lines with him was building something in him he would later miss and crave. Even though he was always surrounded by people, he struggled with a horrible sense of loneliness. He tried hard at first to ignore the calling he had always sensed over his life. He experimented with different hobbies and sought out exploits that might open some sense of completion to that end for him, but he found none. He became incredibly unstable—in one moment, he would be laughing and joking, then suddenly he would turn to depression or uncontrollable fits of rage. He was frustrated and angry, and it is difficult to say if it was all just him, or if that demon was trying to rip him apart from the inside to keep him from his destiny. He was aware of it from time to time and even knew it by name, although to this day he refuses to acknowledge it by saying that name. It was at a party late one night when things turned in an unexpected direction in his life. Up until that night, he was surrounded by an ethereal darkness that anyone who knew him recognized about him. Some would say you could feel Craig walk into the room before you ever saw him. This was still true of him today, but for different reasons.

The party was for his longtime friend Deanna's twenty-first birthday. He had been drinking and getting high most of the evening. Deanna's cousin Grace showed up later in the evening. Grace was beautiful and had a presence about her that somehow lit up the room. Deanna jokingly yelled when she arrived, "Craig, my cousin is off limits!" Craig had known Deanna for many years and had met Grace on several occasions. He had noticed that she never smoked or drank, but he had never thought too much about why that might be true. It wasn't too long before she came up, hugged him, and they began catching up with each other. Grace was very intelligent and could hold her own in a conversation on a wide variety of topics. Eventually, the question came up concerning the reason why she did not get high or drink at these kind of gatherings. Craig was shocked to hear that it was her relationship with God that kept her from doing it. To this day, he could not remember any specifics from the conversation at that point. He remembered that she spoke about God as if he was a person whom she had actual interaction with. This intrigued him and drew him deeper into the conversation. People gradually left the party, and Craig's buzz eventually wore off, but at 3:00 a.m. he found himself still engaged in the conversation. Over his lifetime, many people had invited him to church, tried to hand him Bible tracts and passingly tried to lead him to God. He ignored all those attempts and laughingly brushed them off. Grace was merely sharing the various ways that she believed God interacted personally with her, and he could not get enough. It was near the end of that conversation that she asked him the question he would later say changed his life forever.

Grace asked, "From the time you wake up to the time you go to bed at night being 100 percent of your time, what percentage of that time would you say you are truly at peace within yourself?"

At the time, his answer was easy, "Zero percent, I am miserable and I hate my life."

It was a little surprising to him how easy it was for him to admit that to Grace in this moment.

Her next question, when coupled with the first one, set many things in motion for him. "What if I could promise you 100 percent peace?"

The thought that total peace was even possible sounded ridiculous to him. He almost entirely rejected the implications of that question no sooner than it had escaped her lips. "You can't make that promise."

His sharp reply seemed to have no effect on her at all. She smiled lightly at him and simply said, "I can't, but my God can."

She then asked if she could lead him in a prayer that would help him take the first step in a relationship with God similar to hers. He agreed to it, and he repeated the prayer she presented to him. He felt nothing different in the moment. She told him that was normal, and she suggested a visit with her dad might help him sort out how to move beyond some of the baggage he was bringing to the table.

The party was on a Friday night, and it was nearly five o'clock in the morning on Saturday when the conversation came to a close. Craig slept well when he finally got home. He woke up around one in the afternoon the next day, refreshed and deep in thought about his encounter with Grace the night before. He decided that once he got moving, he would follow her suggestion and go visit her dad later. He sensed that a change of some kind had taken place, but he had no way of identifying what it was. Something had been birthed in him the moment he recited that prayer the night before, but he didn't know what.

That elusive lightness that had sparked within him that night was hope.

CHAPTER 8

Eye Contact

Craig's dad had taught him at an early age, "If you want to have an interesting conversation with someone, go and talk to the person sitting in the room by themselves." This had proven true for him more times than he could count. He had set a goal to have a spiritual conversation with a stranger at least once a week. He was at the gym, it was Friday afternoon, and he had just finished his workout. He whispered a prayer to himself and looked around the room for a person working out alone.

Misty joined a gym every time she moved to a new place. She was disciplined and worked out faithfully four days a week. It was not practical for her to own exercise equipment and drag it with her every time she moved, because her profession kept her moving around a lot. Each gym has its own atmosphere, and Misty had learned to recognize the ones whose clientele were more interested in staying in shape than finding a date. She had met some strong and interesting people along the way, and she was not antisocial. She just saw meeting new people as secondary to being sure she completed her exercise routine. Her current contract was elaborate and was going to require that she stay in the area for several months. She had already been living there a couple months and had yet to find a job she could use as a front for the income from her current contract. The right opportunity usually presented itself, but she had been here long enough that securing a job was on her short list of things she needed to get accomplished. There were still a couple people she recognized as regulars at the gym she had not spoken to yet, and she had not ruled out the possibility that one of them might know of the perfect opportunity she was looking for.

Craig had overcome a great many things to be where he was in life. He was the pastor of a thriving church with a few very successful outreach programs in place. He had been married to his wife for nineteen years, and they had a wonderful relationship. Both of his children were grown and were out on their own. His prayer and devotional life were solid, and he was spiritually strong enough that the grace of God covered his remaining shortcomings. He had one weakness that continued to be his "thorn in the flesh": women. He loved his wife but found himself continually distracted by the beautiful women around him on a daily basis. Early in his marriage and before his entry into the ministry, he had to confess a couple affairs to his wife. It was a rough time, but she forgave him and decided to stick it out. In so doing, she had bought his undying loyalty for life, but that did not change the fact that he had daily distractions to deal with. He kept open and honest communication with his wife concerning these struggles and had developed a couple of strong accountability brothers that he met with regularly to be sure his weakness would not get the best of him. There was way too much to lose at this time in his life and too many lives would be affected in a negative way. He had built up some strength over time and could usually talk with women and maintain an appropriate conversation with them, but he had to work hard to keep his thought life under control.

He had noticed the new Asian woman that had joined the gym about a month or two earlier but had held off talking to her mainly because she was so strikingly beautiful that he wanted to be sure he could keep his conversation and thoughts where they needed to be before he did so. He had caught himself stealing glances at her either directly or through many of the mirrors all over the gym workout area. She usually worked out alone on the machines, but he had seen her hit the free weights as well from time to time. She was very strong in spite of her small frame, and she moved with what seemed like a feline grace that seemed odd considering her apparent physical strength. He had been a member of the gym for a couple years now. His membership was a gift from one of his accountability brothers to help him work on his "temple." He had made a few good relationships here during that time and through one of those acquaintances had learned that the woman's name was Misty. He had whispered a prayer and scanned the room, looking for someone to talk with, and in that moment he felt what he believed to be a slight push from within to finally go meet and talk with Misty.

Misty had just come to the end of her workout as Craig approached her. She recognized him as one of the other regulars at the gym and had never shared more than a greeting in passing with him. She had learned from others that he was a pastor at some big church on the other side of town. In the brief conversations she had overheard or been part of concerning him, she found that everyone respected him and that he had a good name in the community. His church had a couple of outreach programs in place to help the poor and hungry, and it also operated a Christian school and day care center. He had done some marriage counseling for one couple that worked out at the gym together, and they spoke very highly of his methods, although they shared that those methods were somewhat unorthodox. She had noticed that although he appeared to be very outgoing and approachable, that he seemed to be avoiding talking to her for some reason. She dismissed it though and figured that she would meet him soon enough. Of all the other regulars at this gym, it was Craig she decided that would be the most likely to know of any good local job opportunities. If he had not approached her, she would have likely sought him out in the near future.

He smiled as he approached and extended his hand for a handshake, saying, "You're Misty…right?"

She shook hands with him and affirmed, saying, "Yes, and you are Pastor Craig…right? I have heard some of the others talking about you."

He jokingly replied, "Well, don't believe everything that you hear."

Misty answered, "Well, *most* of it has been good."

Craig took a seat next to her on the bench and asked if she had a few minutes to chat. She told him that she had just finished working out. Craig had also finished, so the two agreed to split up, hit the showers, and meet up again on the chairs out in the lobby to chat for a little while.

As he headed off to the showers, Craig could not help but think about Misty's unbelievable hand strength. He had already noticed that she was very strong in spite of her build, but as he walked to the showers, he could still feel the handshake she put on him. Her hands were freakishly strong. There was another small thing he had noticed about her. She maintained eye contact. Craig saw it as a sign of respect to look a person in the eye when you speak to them. (It also helped him keep his eyes from wandering in certain situations.) He found that most people, even ones who seemed to be outwardly confident in other ways, would not maintain eye contact in a conversation. Misty on the other hand, locked eyes with him as he approached and kept eye contact during the whole exchange, as brief as it was.

Misty also noted that Pastor Craig maintained eye contact during their brief conversation. She had found that no matter how virtuous a man claimed to be, she would still catch his eyes looking her body over. It was difficult to know if Craig was just that disciplined or if the exchange was short enough that his eyes did not have time to wander, but he had gained some respect from her in that short conversation.

It was about twenty minutes before both of them emerged from the locker rooms and sat opposite each other in two of the plush chairs in the lobby to chat. Misty was mildly amused to see that Pastor Craig came out of the locker room dressed in jeans, tennis shoes, and a black T-shirt with a Batman emblem on it. Any ministers she had previously seen or had contact with always wore dress clothes. She appreciated his authenticity or, at the very least, what that seemed to imply about his comfortable self-confidence. Apparently, he did not feel a need to dress the part. He took a seat in the chair opposite from where she was sitting.

Misty commented on his shirt. "Batman?"

Without missing a beat, Craig replied, "Sin causes people to commit crime. As a pastor, I help people deal with that sin, which subsequently keeps them from committing crimes. So that makes me a crime fighter. I am Batman."

Misty chuckled. "Solid logic, but doesn't being an eccentric millionaire conflict with the humility of being a pastor?"

Craig paused for moment to consider his answer to that question. In the moment, it was difficult to discern if she was playing along or testing his character. He needed to formulate an answer that would satisfy both. "Yeah, but the real conflict is when I beat them and tie them up. You know all pastors are supposed to be timid pacifists."

Misty laughed at his answer and commented, "You are not like any other minister I have ever met before."

Craig nodded and answered, "Yeah, I get that a lot."

She was amazed at how disarming Craig was. She immediately felt comfortable talking to him. He had a sharp sense of humor and was a very intense person. He talked as if he was giving the highlights to some professional ball game, and his emphasis made the mundane events of daily life spring to new life. His spiritual journey was very interesting. She could tell from listening to him that he enjoyed telling the story. She also decided that it was probably intentional that he began sharing his own story first. It was not a prideful thing, but more that he wanted to probe for whatever common ground he might have with you by putting himself out there first. He shared for about twenty minutes, with pauses to affirm whatever common ground they shared, and then sat back in his chair. Misty almost felt as if she needed to catch her breath by the time he was done.

After a brief pause, Craig said, "So tell me about Misty. What is your story?"

Misty had worked a great deal on a believable backstory and told basically the same one everywhere she went. It was a mixture of both fact and fiction. As a child, she did spend some time in an orphanage, and it was true that she never knew her parents. They had turned her over to the orphanage as an infant. The Americans had adopted her at an early enough age that she only had a few brief memories of that orphanage, and those were unpleasant memories. She skipped over the adoption part and usually shared that she was at the orphanage until she was eighteen. The Rising Sun adoption agency was a horrible place, and although most of her stories about the place were fabricated, she imagined that they could be true for any of the kids who remained there. The fabricated stories were a sufficient springboard to explain her desire to travel the world and get as far from there as possible. Her story was that she read a lot of books and studied several different languages throughout her teenage years in preparation for those travels.

She claimed to have retired early from a career in commercial real estate. Her job, as she conveyed it, was to match clients who were either buying or selling commercial space. It was a good way to explain all the traveling she did, and also how she had plenty of expendable income.

She explained it like this: "Say you are a Chinese businessman, and you are looking to expand somewhere in the United States. My job was to do some market research and find a few good locations that would be suitable for that expansion. I met with property owners here in the States and put together a portfolio for my client that included pricing and contact information for several potential expansion sites. When my client found a property they were interested in, I negotiated the deal and settled all the paperwork. I worked in the field for nearly ten years and negotiated deals all over the world. I usually made a great deal of money in those transactions, and after some smart investing, I was able to retire early."

Craig listened intently, and afterward he asked, "So what are you doing now?"

Misty answered, "Not really anything at the moment. I suppose I am looking for something different and challenging. Money is not really an issue, so if I find an opportunity that sounds interesting, I will probably give it a shot. For the last few years, I guess you could say I have just been traveling and collecting college degrees."

Craig was fascinated with Misty's story. He spent some time asking her about the different places she had visited all over the world, and before he knew it, they had been sitting there chatting for nearly two hours. Every once in a while, you meet a person and you instantly sense a connection to them. It is as if you have known them your whole life. This conversation turned out to be one of that kind. Two people from entirely different lives and backgrounds came together and chatted, and as a result, the seeds for a growing friendship were planted. Toward the end of the conversation, Craig had brought the conversation back around and asked what college degrees Misty held. It was an impressive list. Of particular interest to him was her degree in world history. His history teacher at the Christian school his church ran was going to be taking medical leave for a round of chemotherapy, and he knew they were in desperate need of a replacement. It was difficult to find teachers for the school because the budget was limited, and they could not compete with the wages offered by the public or other private schools.

He decided to mention it to her to see if she was interested. "Hey, I heard you mention a degree in world history. We run a Christian school at my church, and our history teacher is going on medical leave for a round of chemotherapy. Would you be interested in doing some teaching?"

Her education in world history was mainly necessary because of her travels, she also needed to know something about the topic should her job require her to know historical details of the area she was in. Shifts in political movement were also important knowledge to have. She had never considered teaching as a possibility before. It would be a challenge to translate what she knew into course work that she could teach, but she was confident it could be done. The best part was that no one would be looking for a professional killer to be teaching history at a Christian school. She decided in the moment to give it a shot.

Craig's cell phone rang as she was thinking it over. Judging by his part in the conversation, she figured out that it was his wife calling to see if he was coming home for dinner. He smiled briefly in Misty's direction and told his wife to keep it warm and that he would be on his way shortly. He hung up from the call and asked, "So what do you think?"

She answered, "Well, I have never taught before, but I could pop in, look the textbook over, and give it a shot. How soon would you need me?"

"Well, the sooner I can secure someone for the position, the better it will be for Julianna. That way she can focus on her treatments and know we have it covered. She doesn't start for a couple weeks yet, so she could work with you until then to see if you could pick it up."

Misty agreed and asked what he needed her to do.

Craig said, "Well, I will give you one of my cards, and if you can, email me your résumé some time before this Sunday afternoon. I will call the school's board of directors together and talk it over with them. If everything falls into place, you could pop in Monday afternoon, and I will show you around and see if it is a good fit for everyone."

Misty took his card and told him she would send the email as soon as she got home. With that, they shook hands again and parted company. Misty watched Craig half jog to his car and was surprised to see him pull away in a nice red two-door sports car. She liked him. He was a great guy, and she had enjoyed their conversation. She gathered that he was a powerful and driven man. He spoke with passion and conviction but mixed it with his own unorthodox frivolity, which was very intriguing to her. She had guessed correctly that he would be her best chance at securing some kind of employment, but things had worked out far better than she had anticipated if this opportunity worked out for her.

Craig was happy to be headed home and could not wait to tell his wife about the encounter with Misty. The possibility that he had found a substitute for Julianna was an added bonus. He found Misty to be a fascinating person, but he had an odd sense that there was something elusive about her he could not figure out. It seemed odd that a commercial real estate agent and student would be so freakishly strong, but he just attributed it to the fact that she had a tough upbringing at the orphanage. She was strikingly beautiful, and there were parts of the conversation where he really had to fight to keep his eye contact with her. When he got home and joined his wife at the dinner table, the first words out of his mouth were, "You are not going to believe this!" They had both experienced so much supernatural provision from God in the past though, that he knew she would not be as excited about the news as he was.

The board looked Misty's résumé over and was overwhelmed by her work history and education. It would really be a blessing if someone of such high quality and worldly experience was willing to teach at their humble little Christian school. They eagerly and unanimously voted to give her the shot at teaching if she wanted it. Craig called her that Sunday evening and set up for her to come by the school the next day around noon to show her around. He told her that the board was excited and that they had unanimously and enthusiastically voted to extend the position to her if she wanted it. He joked that she should not answer too quickly before she came and met the kids. "You might turn and run after that," he said jokingly. She assured him that she had been to some of the darker and more dangerous parts of the world and that some Christian school kids were of no concern.

Quite a buzz had spread concerning the arrival of this new substitute teacher Pastor Craig had met at the gym, and several people who did not normally have business during the day at the church had found a reason to be there. Misty had dressed conservatively in a black suit and black heels. She felt the eyes of several people watching her as she approached, which she decided might be her own preconceived notions about what kind of people she might encounter at this church and school. She was pleasantly surprised at how friendly the people were as Craig walked her around the facility. It was a lot larger than she had imagined, and along with the sanctuary and school, many of the programs they had for the community were operated on these grounds. He had saved giving her the tour of the school last because he wanted to wait until lunch was over and the kids had all returned to class. He walked her through the halls and explained the layout of the classrooms. The school started at preschool age and went all the way through eighth grade. There were plans to build and add a high school program, but with budget issues and state requirements, Craig said it was a year or two off. He paused at one particular door before opening it and told her, "This is Julianna's class, the one you would be taking over."

Julianna was at the front of the room, teaching from the dry-erase board as they walked in. She smiled at them and paused from her work for a moment. There was some general chatter going on in the room typical of middle school kids who are distracted and waiting for the final bell to ring. The moment Craig and Misty entered the room, a quiet hush fell over the kids that was so intense it was as if all the air had sucked out of the room. Misty had no experience in the classroom, but Craig and Julianna were both astonished at the sudden quiet that had fallen over the room. Julianna reached out to shake hands with Misty and said, "I could use some of whatever that magic is you have that made them so quiet." Misty looked the room over, smiled, and said, "Whenever I figure out what it is, I would be happy to pass some on to you."

The first thing Misty noticed about Julianna was her beautiful blue-green eyes. She noticed that she was slightly pale and secretly wondered how sick she might be feeling on the inside. If she was experiencing any discomfort, you could not tell from her appearance. She was a happy and vibrant person and spoke with a quiet pleasant tone that was actually soothing to Misty like the purr of a kitten. The three of them spoke briefly, and Julianna handed a copy of the history book to Misty for her to take home and look over. She had also made Misty a copy of her lesson plans, but she added that Misty was free to do her own thing as long as the units that had to be covered were taken care of. The entire time the three of them spoke, the kids looked on silently. After a few minutes, Craig and Misty turned to leave the room. Misty headed out first. As Craig walked out behind her, he looked back at Julianna. She mouthed the words "I *like* her!" to Craig, and he smiled back at her as he shut the door. Of course, after a few moments, the chatter in the room resumed, but at a slightly higher pitch than before Craig and Misty had entered the room.

Craig walked Misty out to her car and asked her what her initial impression was concerning the facility and the teaching position. He was trying not to sound desperate, but the fact that Julianna was happy with her carried a lot of weight. Her husband, Paul, was a longtime friend of his. It was devastating news when they diagnosed Julianna with cancer. Craig had reassured Paul that a cancer diagnosis was not the death sentence it used to be, that many treatments were available, and that new ones were being experimented with all the time. It was still hard news to deal with, and everyone knew it was a hard road ahead. If Misty accepted the job, it would help Julianna to rest easy that her class was taken care of. She loved the kids, and teaching them was a calling that she took very seriously.

Misty answered, "Well, give me a week to look the materials over and figure out some kind of game plan, then I will work with Julianna starting Monday next week…if that works for you."

She shared that the facility was much larger than she imagined and that she was slightly impressed that all this was the result of one man's vision and direction. She commented on how welcome she had felt by all the people she had met that day and admitted that she had expected them to be more stereotypical. Craig assured her that he knew what she meant and that the first face you see on some people might not be their most common. Aside from that, he spoke very proudly of the community he believed God had assembled there under his leadership. She agreed that this was a good place and affirmed that the respect she had heard some of the people at the gym extended to him was well deserved. With that, she shook hands with him, got in her car, and pulled away.

Misty had been all over the world and encountered all types of religious beliefs along with their adherents. The Christians she had experienced in other parts of the world were usually devout and genuinely loving people. They engaged in pure and honest acts of servanthood and, most times, did so at personal risk to themselves and loved ones. American Christians, on the other hand, were for the most part the bottom of the barrel. They seemed to have a sense of entitlement and were easily manipulated by their media and politicians' agendas. They were either notoriously legalistic and intolerant or complacently relaxed and unengaged. America has its own Christian subculture with its own phraseology, music, and merchandise (which Misty had come to call "Jesus Junk"). She remembered several conversations she had with William before her training moved outside of the facility and out into the world. She knew he was a Christian, and it was evident in his character. She was surprised once she got out into the world to find that not all Christians worked on their character as he did. It had been decades since she had seen him, but she still thought of him from time to time.

She was honestly impressed at what Craig had been able to accomplish. He was humble of course, and attributed the success of the ministries encompassed by Thicker Than Water to the help and dedication of others. She learned from talking to him that the original vision for the facilities and the ministry was his alone. He had worked hard to find other like-minded people who shared his vision and were tenacious enough to actually build it. Julianna's husband, Paul, played a large part in bringing it all together, and she learned they had been friends for a long time. She gathered from the conversation with Craig that Paul had done a great deal of traveling as well and figured they might have seen some of the same places.

She looked the textbook and lesson plans over and jotted down some ideas on how to enhance the information. She decided it might be a slight advantage to teach about different places in the world that she had actually visited. The next unit was about the rise of Rome. No amount of showing pictures and talking about the coliseums could match actually standing in their ruins and hearing the sounds of Rome echo within their walls. You could really understand how overwhelming it might have been to witness the games there when you saw the immensity of those ruins first-hand. As she considered how those details might enhance the delivery of the lessons, she decided that she might actually enjoy teaching.

CHAPTER 9
Unlikely Source of Light (Part Two)

After this day, Craig would tell people that his dog, Loki, spoke to him.

A person will find divine inspiration in the strangest places when their heart is focused on God. He was surprised at first how the epiphany came to him through Loki. But after further contemplation, it made perfect sense. Craig loved to tell people the story of how he got Loki. He loved that dog more than most people and considered him to be a gift from God.

A lady he worked with bred boxers. One day, she had brought in a box of two-day-old puppies to show off. She was taking them to the vet that day to get their tails bobbed. Another girl from there had brought one of the puppies to the door of his office. She asked what he told people was the dumbest question anyone had ever asked, "Do you want to hold a puppy?"

Of course, he did.

He snapped a picture of the one he was holding and texted it to Kay with the caption, "Can I keep it?" Kay was strict about the fact that they already had one dog, which was advanced in years and difficult to care for, and that they were a one-dog household. When he eventually handed the puppy back, he asked how much they were selling for. At $250 each, any hope he had for adding a boxer puppy to the family dissipated. Before he handed the puppy back, he said a prayer over it. He asked that it quickly recover from the pain of getting its tail cut off and that this particular one would wind up in a good, loving home.

About six or seven weeks later, the same girl who brought the puppy to his office came to him and told him that the lady who bred the boxers said if he wanted one, he could have it for free. Kay was coming to have lunch with him that day, so he immediately tried to figure out how he could make it work. Labor Day was a couple weeks away, and he had scheduled that Friday off as well to create a four-day weekend. His suggestion to Kay that day was that he could pick the puppy up on Friday and try it for the weekend. If it didn't work out, he could give it back that following Tuesday. He *knew* that if he could just get that puppy in her hands it would be a done deal. He had arranged to meet the lady at her home that Friday and pick one, but plans changed, and it worked out that she would pick one and meet him at the office to drop it off. Craig had always suspected that Kay relented because of how happy that dog had made him. (He later admitted and repented for being manipulative about it.) The bigger dog they already had was named Thor. The obvious name for the new mischievous boxer puppy troubling him was Loki. It was not until a few weeks later that Craig had found the picture of the puppy he texted to Kay months earlier. By comparing the markings from the dog in that picture against the markings on Loki, he figured out that he had gotten the puppy he prayed for. Once he realized that, he associated that dog with the love of God every time he looked into those comically bulged-out eyes and sagging-jawed face.

The first couple months in his new home, Loki's feet rarely touched the floor in the evenings. Craig would settle into his favorite chair, and Loki would be cradled in his arms, sleeping like a baby. He stubbornly refused to sleep in his cage overnight. Craig and Kay tried everything. They moved the cage into their room. Craig even spent one night sleeping on the floor with his finger in the cage. Loki would sleep resting against his finger, but if he moved to try and get up to go to bed, Loki would start whining and barking again. Finally, in a tired night of frustration, Craig got Loki out of the cage and laid him in bed between himself and Kay. To this day, that is where he slept—in bed, right between Craig and Kay. Inevitably, Loki had real problems with separation anxiety. He had to be caged during the day while they were at work. For a long time, he had rubbed a raw spot on the top of his head from trying to get out of the cage during the day. After several lectures from Kay, she finally convinced Craig that his constant cradling and pampering of the dog was doing Loki more harm than good and that Loki needed some independence. It took some time, but he gradually adjusted to being in the cage during the day, but he still had the small scar on his head from that raw spot.

Thor already had issues with his back legs and hips before Loki joined the family. He was a great dog that had been an anchor in the family through some difficult times. He was primarily annoyed by the puppy, and with the occasional deep bark, he kept Loki at a distance. Shortly after Loki joined the family, Thor's condition worsened to the point that he had to be put to sleep. It was a very sad time. Craig, Kay, and the local vet never figured out if it was a genetic issue or if Loki just terribly missed his big brother. He kept getting sick and could not hold down his food. Loki had a team of veterinarians run a battery of tests on him, but they could not find anything wrong. The "free" dog wound up costing around $1,000 in medical bills. Craig did some internet research and found a natural dog food that Loki was able to digest, and shortly after his first birthday, the problem seemed to go away.

Loki had his own seat at the dinner table now. He put his head down on the table when Craig or Kay said the dinner prayer. Craig gave him Saltine crackers and called them his "dinner crackers." In addition to his special dog food, the crackers helped him put on some weight, and at just over two years old, he was happy, healthy, and active.

Craig usually did his devotions at night after Kay went to bed. He enjoyed the dark and quiet of night and found that there was less likelihood of an interruption of his devotional time if he did it at night. Loki would usually join him in his office and lie quietly on the couch until his devotional time was over and then follow him to bed. This particular night, Craig was frustrated and perplexed as he began his devotions.

That hope he received after the night Grace prayed with him had carried through an amazing spiritual journey. God was real to him. He had conceived of the idea of Thicker than Water Ministries early on in his walk. It was a fluid kind of vision that had developed over the years, but at the same time, it was very clear to him. In his heart, he could see the kind of community that Christianity could become. He could sense the change in the lives of the people such a community would create. He drove himself mad by writing constantly about the vision and the various observations he had made about how to improve upon the existing Christian subculture.

Craig had spent money trying to self-publish a couple books based on those writings. He had created several video sermons and posted them on YouTube. A good friend of his had actually built him a website for the ministry, which gave him a place to post all the writings and videos. He worked hard in whatever time he could find to try to promote the ministry and the vision that he felt God had given him. The problem, as it always was, was finances. Their combined income was barely enough to cover his and Kay's basic bills. He spent any extra that could be milked out on the ministry, but he never seemed to have enough to bring the vision to life. He was angry and frustrated, and the weight of all his blocked goals had brought him to a place where he had seriously began to doubt not just his calling but his entire walk. It was a dark place.

It was in that spirit that he had entered into his devotional time that night. Loki had walked in with him as he usually did and settled into the couch across the room from him. Craig fell back into his chair, and with tears in his eyes, he cried out to God in desperation.

"Jesus, I have done everything I know to do. I have prayed, preached, and exhausted myself trying to build this ministry—*your ministry* as you have placed it in my heart! I am tired of our financial situation. I am frustrated with the state of your church. I don't understand why you seem uninterested when it comes to the work I am trying to complete for you. Work that *you* have laid so deeply upon my heart! I am giving up tonight if you do not speak to me! I know it is never you and that the problem is always me. I am starting to think that I have judged wrongly all along and that I have built this entire ministry on my own effort. *Please!* Speak to me in a way that is clear to me that I can understand."

He held his head down in silence for several moments to listen and then decided that no answer was forthcoming. So he dried his eyes and looked up. Loki was on the couch across the room from him. He usually slept and had to be nudged when devotional time was over. This time, he was lying on the couch, but when Craig looked up, Loki was awake and staring intently at him. He swore there was something in Loki's eyes indicating that the dog somehow knew the anguish he was experiencing. After a few moments of staring at each other, Loki let out a small bark at Craig, then lay back down and closed his eyes.

And there was the epiphany.

Loki had no idea what Craig was doing when he followed him into that office. He just wanted to be wherever Craig was. He always positioned himself on that couch in a way that he could see where Craig was sitting, either in his chair or at his desk. He didn't move until he was nudged that it was time to move. He was content to just rest in the company of his master until it was time to move. Craig had worked hard to get everything he had in life. He was passionate and driven. Whenever there was a void in leadership, he immediately jumped in. He always felt a sense that the Holy Spirit was driving him. But in this moment, he realized that maybe Christ was telling him that it was time to stop fighting at last and let him do the work. In the same way Loki just wanted to rest in Craig's presence, maybe what God wanted was for Craig to rest in his presence and wait to be nudged? Maybe the idea was that it was time for Craig to rest in a way that he could see where God was, but wait for him to do the work?

Then, the realization hit him that it was entirely possible that God had answered his earlier prayer and allowed this little boxer to come into his life just for this moment. He knew the desperation and frustration would be building and that it would take a special kind of answer to push out the negativity all these years of independent fighting had built. Jesus knew that in this moment he didn't have to come down in a chariot of flame with a burning scroll. All he needed to do was move on the heart of a little boxer dog to bark attentively at just the right moment. His prayer had been that Christ would speak to him in a way that he could understand. There was so much going on in his life that he did not understand, but he understood that little bark.

Loki…spoke to him.

The next day, he received a call from his accountant friend, Bill. Bill had a client who was back from traveling abroad. The client was looking for a good charity to pour some funds into. He had told the client briefly about Thicker than Water Ministries and piqued his interest. Bill was calling to set up a meeting with him and Kay to introduce them so they could talk more about it. He suggested that Bill bring him over for dinner, and they set a date and time.

CHAPTER 10
Ms. Misty Crosses the Line

In comparison with being a schoolteacher, being a professional killer was easy.

There were about thirty middle school-aged kids sitting in her class. She had been teaching the class for several months. She was surprised how naturally being a teacher came to her. These inner-city kids were tough and seemed to fit the whole "city kid" stereotype. This was not what you would consider the stereotypical classroom though despite its urban setting. Sure, the kids were all wearing the culturally accepted urban wear. Hairstyles in the room also reflected the focus on individuality that was common to youth culture. The difference is that the students were sitting quietly, stone still, and paying close attention to their teacher. Well, all the students except for one—there is one in every class.

Pete's dad is an alcoholic. Pete's family life is the stereotypical model of one who is led by a lazy, binge-drinking dad. His clothing looks worn and wrinkled, and he looks as if he has not showered in a few days. The other kids pick on him, so he has developed a bitter hatred for every human being on Earth. Pete's dad was exceptionally violent this morning, so Pete was in a hurry to get out of the house. The nasty purple-and-black swelling under his right eye seems to indicate that he did not get out of the house fast enough. Pete's focus has been out the window, counting tiles in the ceiling, looking for shapes in the pattern on the floor tiles, and everywhere but the teacher. He has gotten bored with all this, and now he wants a new setting to explore.

"Missus Misty, can ah go to da restroom?" he asks.

"Did someone say something?" she replies. "I don't think it's possible that I heard an actual voice in here, because nobody raised their hand for permission to speak."

With a look of bitter indignation, Pete throws his hand in the air and waves it around in mock urgency. "Missus Misty, ah gotta go poop really bad," he says, and he adds a little smirk because he managed to get a small burst of laughter from his classmates.

Misty hides her small smile so as not to encourage more disruptive behavior, and she knows Pete does not have to use the restroom. She has been watching him out of the corner of her eye and saw him shifting in his seat since shortly after class had begun. She was shocked and hurt when she saw the latest shiner on his right eye and had decided to ask him about it after class to see which excuse he would offer up this time. She surprisingly has grown to love the kids, and they know it, which is why they behave and show her the quiet reverence they do in her classroom. She is not foolish enough to ignore the fact that the boys in her class are mesmerized and most likely undressing her in their young puberty-tortured minds as well. She dresses very conservatively to keep from adding to that particular distraction. Her attention is continually drawn to Pete because he is the one student she cannot seem to connect with despite how well she is received by all the other students. She goes to great lengths to be firm and fair, but she tries secretively to go easier on Pete whenever she can. She feels for him, and she knows all too well, what he is dealing with at home. Down inside, she wonders how long she can sit by and watch this child's life continually destroyed by his abusive alcoholic father. It sickens her.

"Sounds like an emergency, kid. You better go take care of that!" she says, and she motions for him to go ahead and take his trip to the restroom. The class lets out a small giggle as Pete exits the class. A stern look restores order in the class, and she continues her lesson.

It is not long before the bell rings, indicating that her last class of the day is over. As the students stand and excitedly exit the class, she calls after Pete to ask about his bruise.

"Hey, Petey, I need you to stay over for just a few moments so I can go over what you missed during your trip to the restroom… okay?" she says.

Pete makes his way to the desk and waits for the others to leave the classroom. He has an unusual sense of urgency about him today, and she notices him glancing out the door as if he is in a hurry to leave. She glosses over the few minor details that Pete missed during his trip to the restroom and then inquires about the bruise.

"So, Petey, that's a nasty bruise under your eye…"

She anticipates another story about falling off the swing or slipping down the stairs, like all the other stories before. She is an expert on reading people, and she senses that there is something different about Pete today. Pete's eyes tear up, and his focus is almost completely on leaving the room. Misty is a cold and emotionless killer, but she was not ready for the brutal honesty she was about to be blasted with by this troubled student.

"Mah dad hits me, Missus Misty. Ah know that you know he does 'cause you're very smart. Ah really don't have time tah talk though 'cause things got really bad this mornin'. Mah aunt is s'posed to be pickin' me up after school tuhday 'cause Dad put Mom in the hospital last night when he got home from work. That's how I got this black eye… Ah jumped on him to save my mommy. Mah aunt says it's just for a few days until Dad's temper goes back down. She don't realize though that Dad's temper nevuh goes down. So anyways, don't be mad if I don't come back to class… Ah'm sure gonna miss you…"

Razormist, the stone-cold and emotionless killer, chokes back the tears long enough to smile and hug Pete goodbye. She looks in his eyes and cannot help but drink in the pain that this strong young boy has endured.

"I am really going to miss you too, Petey, and that was a really brave thing you did trying to protect your mommy. She is lucky to have you as a son. Someday, your dad will also realize how lucky he is… Trust me."

Pete says goodbye and is off in a flash to go find his aunt waiting outside. Misty closes the door calmly, walks over to her desk, sits down, and cries into her hands for almost twenty minutes. In an instant, the tears are turned off, and she has her focus back…razor-sharp. She never expected to feel so strongly for these kids when she agreed to take the job. She never thought those strong feelings would drive her to consider the course of action she was now preparing to take. By definition, being a professional killer was always business and never personal. She knows that this course of action could expose her and reveal her carefully guarded secret identity. Pete has no one else to turn to though. Surely, it was for some greater purpose she had been brought into his life. She had been doing a lot of thinking on spiritual issues lately. She still had not discovered who was responsible for leaking to her last target and alerting them about the hit. She had gotten so caught up in preparing for her lessons that it had been weeks since she had attempted any real investigation on the topic. She also enjoyed being part of the overall ministry. She was continually impressed by the people she encountered in her daily life as a result of her involvement with Thicker Than Water. People naturally gravitated to this community of believers, and it was impressive how quickly Craig and his team discovered their areas of giftedness and plugged them into it. At times, she felt bad for her intentional deception, and she looked down on herself for the fact that the ministry had no use for a professional killer. There was one thing she could use her particular skill set for though. She alone was uniquely gifted to end this poor young boy's suffering.

She opened the file drawer of her desk and fingered her way through the files until she came to Pete's folder. She raised it slightly out of the drawer and took the slightest peek at the home address. She stole an additional glance at the name listed as the boy's father, "Ralph." She grabbed her briefcase from the desk and headed out of the classroom for the day.

"He will realize how lucky he is, Pete. Trust me."

CHAPTER 11
Dinner and Conversation

God has a plan.

He connects people across lines that we would never be able to anticipate in order to execute that plan. Most Christians draw lines and boundaries in places where God does not. Classifications like "sacred" and "secular" are not as easily defined in the working out of God's plan the way most who would like to consider themselves his people claim them to be. We are flawed people living in a broken world. Christ works best through our brokenness. While we waste time in our spiritual growth trying to achieve milestones we establish for ourselves, Christ waits for us to yield to him so he can use us as we are. We sing "Just as I Am" in our worship services, but most of the time we do not worship him in that way.

Craig and Paul were coworkers in a warehouse. Paul's parents passed away and left him a fortune. His parents were devout followers of Christ who not only prayed for Paul's prosperity but were fortunate enough to be able to provide for it. Paul was not a Christian when he received that inheritance from his parents. (Much like when we are born again and we receive ours.) He had decided to travel the world and find himself. His heart was moved by the suffering he witnessed in other parts of the world during his travels. Through the influence of his financial adviser, Bill, that movement in his heart became the foundation for his salvation. Bill led Paul to the Lord during a cell phone conversation. It really is that simple.

Long before he became a Christian, Craig always had a higher sense of purpose than what his upbringing would indicate. There was one summer that food was so scarce in his home that he and his younger sister had resorted to eating dry cat food. For a long time, Craig hated his heritage and worked in as many ways as he could to gain the prestige he felt he deserved. His heart yearned for greatness and popularity, and the longer he lived with lack, the more frustrated and angry he became. His blocked goals led him to porn addiction, alcoholism, drug abuse, and even worse, demonic possession. It was hopelessness that led Craig into his relationship with Christ. It was not until after he had learned several harsh lessons on humbleness and humility that God awakened that sense of purpose in him with renewed focus. This came in the form of the idea for Thicker than Water Ministries. Craig first envisioned it as a church. Over the years, as he grew spiritually, the vision for his ministry developed as well. He was continually frustrated at his lack of ability to acquire the finances he needed to start the ministry. It was through an epiphany created by a single bark from his dog Loki that he learned the final lesson he needed. It is God's plan. What God originates, God orchestrates. Craig was thinking about building a ministry... God wanted to start a movement.

When Paul gave Craig his car and left to see the world, neither of them thought they would ever see each other again. When Craig stopped in Bill's office to talk about financial planning and trying to build Thicker than Water Ministries, Bill could not have known that Craig and Paul knew each other. Even Paul could sense that Craig was destined to accomplish some great purpose when they worked together, but he had no way of knowing that he would be the one to finance it. All these things were part of God's plan, and all of them were set in motion before any of them could have anticipated what God was going to do. Through Christ, God built a thriving community of unique Christians at Thicker than Water Ministries. The character of the ministry was based upon Craig's strong desire to bring "outsiders" together as a faith-based community, and Paul's heart to use his wealth to ease the suffering of others. As the years progressed, Christ intentionally cultivated a specific spiritual environment through this ministry. He did so for the purpose of reaching one specific soul that otherwise might not have responded to him.

That person had unknowingly stumbled into a place that Christ had skillfully crafted for the purpose of touching their heart in a delicate place. This person had no real family. All they had known was a lifetime of loneliness. God wanted to show his love to that person in a meaningful and life changing way.

That special soul was the professional killer who was internationally known as Razormist.

Misty could never have anticipated the fact that life events were steering her swiftly toward an encounter with a loving God. It would take her years of spiritual growth to understand the elaborate work God had done to cure her loneliness, give her new purpose, and to provide a family for her in order to vividly illustrate his love to her.

When Bill pulled up in Craig's driveway to introduce him to Craig, it was purely to connect two guys who he felt had common goals toward building ministry. No one at this meeting could have anticipated that one day a professional killer would show up at the ministry's doorstep and subsequently be transformed forever.

"Paul?"

"Craig?"

Craig just happened to be looking out the front door when Bill's car pulled up in the driveway, and walked out the door to greet him and his guest. Bill had told him about his millionaire friend and that he was looking for a unique ministry to contribute to. When Paul stepped out of the car, Craig immediately recognized him, and he nearly fell over. Bill had been working with Craig to try and build up some resources toward a unique vision for ministry. Bill thought it was best to just connect the two men and let Craig share the ideas he had for himself. He had known Paul for years and, over that time, had built a strong friendship with him. The ministry Craig had been inspired to create was exactly the kind of thing Paul wanted to be a part of. He was caught completely off guard when it became evident that the two knew each other.

"You guys know each other?"

Kay heard excited murmuring at the driveway out front and went to the door to see what all the fuss was about. She arrived at the door just in time to see Craig excitedly hug the guest Bill had brought for dinner to talk about the ministry. When the men pulled apart from each other, she recognized the other man as Craig's former coworker, Paul.

"Oh my god, Paul?"

"Kay! You're still with this loser?"

Kay hugged Paul and replied, "He's not perfect, but I still love him."

Craig got an expression on his face like he had suddenly remembered something really important. "Paul, come with me, I have something to show you!"

Kay hugged Bill and said hello as Craig led Paul into the house. She could tell that Bill was at a loss for words and took some time to explain to him how the two knew each other as she led him into the house. The house had an attached garage, and Kay knew what Craig wanted to show Paul before her and Bill caught up to them there.

"*No way!* Is this my baby?" Paul asked.

Craig still had the car Paul had given him but, over the years, had made some modifications. Now it sported chrome rims, a state-of-the-art sound system, and a sleek new paint job. Kay left the men to admire the sports car in the garage and went to the kitchen to set the table for dinner. She was happy in her heart because she knew Christ had just shown up. Craig had obsessed about Thicker Than Water over the years, and most of the time, he was angry and frustrated at his seeming lack of progress. She loved that he was a driven man, but at times, his impulsiveness was aggravating. Craig's ideas concerning ministry challenged the traditional patterns of ministry she had grown accustomed to that she was raised with. But over the years, she watched him reach people for Christ that only his approach would work with. Finances were always an issue. The fact that Bill's millionaire friend turned out to be Craig's old friend Paul seemed to indicate that God was ready to bring a blessing that would allow Craig's ministry vision to become a reality. She was both excited and scared.

The four settled down for dinner and listened to stories about the countries Paul had visited and the experiences of his travels. Bill had already heard most of Paul's stories and mostly sat back and enjoyed the family reunion feel of the evening. Craig and Kay listened intently to what seemed like the script to an excellent action movie. Paul had seen and done a lot of things. He had picked up a couple foreign languages along the way. He had looked down the barrel of a gun on a few occasions. He had made several great relationships with interesting people all over the world that he still maintained. They finished dinner, and Kay listened to Paul as she cleared the table and cleaned the dishes. He closed the storytelling time by sharing about his recent date with Julianna. He had a crush on her since middle school and could not believe that she had reentered his life. He felt like the date went well, and they had agreed to see each other again.

After that, Paul said, "So tell me about you guys, and what is this idea you have for a ministry?"

Craig started his story from the last time he saw Paul. "Well, I had an epiphany shortly after you left about starting a different kind of church. You know I have always been different..."

Paul chuckled lightly at that and nodded in approval.

"The idea was to eliminate all the man-made traditions and just build a church that focused more on ways for people to express their natural individuality. I felt an urge to go to seminary, but financially it just did not seem to be an option. I said a very direct prayer at the time. I told God that I was willing to go seminary if that is what he wanted me to do, but that I didn't want to have to work and attend school... I wanted to be able to focus purely on my studies."

Kay had heard Craig tell this story several times. She always cringed within herself when she remembered that time in their marriage. Those events seemed to unfold so suddenly, and they were some of the hardest times they ever experienced. Craig nearly lost his faith a couple times back then, and she had to admit her own faith had been severely tested. God's involvement was evident when they looked back on the whole thing, but not so much in the midst of it all.

Craig continued, "About four months after you left, I injured my back really bad. I ruptured my L4 and L5 discs in my lower back. I was down for almost two years. We had to file bankruptcy on our home. We sold Kay's car. She wound up having to get a job and drove your baby to and from work. I had a red recliner, and other than using the bathroom and showers, I basically lived in that recliner."

Paul winced at this and said, "Well, praise God, you seem to be okay now."

"It was a rough road to recovery," Craig replied and then he continued.

"I received a series of steroid shots in my lower back that basically solved the problem. I lost some range of motion, but for the most part, it got me up out of that recliner. The muscles of my lower back had atrophied, so it took a few months before I could walk upright and pain-free again. One of the best days of my life was the day I carried that red recliner out to the trash!"

Kay added, "That was a victorious day for both of us."

"Well, we filed bankruptcy on the house, so we still needed to find a place to live. On a whim, I applied to the nearest seminary that offered family housing on campus and got accepted. We lived there four years and were able to survive on just Kay's job at a local day care center and the occasional generosity of others. I focused on my studies and got away after almost five years with two degrees. During those years, as a side project, I jotted down every thought I had about that church I wanted to start, but over that time, the vision developed and widened out some. I met new people and saw new needs that the ministry could meet."

Paul was intrigued, and he asked, "How well were your ideas received at seminary? Were you able to establish any contacts there toward building this thing?"

Craig answered, "Yeah, right, that place was far too weighed down in the man-made traditions of the church to hear anything I had to say. I actually had a slight identity crisis during my time there because I was so radically different from everyone around me. The series of events that helped me out of that is an excellent story for another time."

He didn't comment, but Paul was glad that Craig had come out of the experience with his unique personality intact. He always felt that Craig was being driven by some deeper purpose. He had forgotten about Craig's passion while he was away on his travels, but sitting here in front of him was like a breath of fresh air. He couldn't wait to hear the rest of Craig's ideas, but he had already decided that no matter how outlandish they were that he was going to support him.

"I pastored my first church right out of seminary. It was a terrible experience. I spent hundreds of hours in prayer for the growth of that church and the people who attended there. I worked tirelessly to craft original sermons rather than take the easy way like many other pastors and borrow sermon notes from others. I worked long hours—in some cases, far from home—because the church could not pay me full time, and it was the only work I could find that did not conflict with my church responsibilities. My, we worked hard to keep the grass cut, which until the church finally bought a riding mower, at times required hours of push mowing. My wife and I were engaged in the community and made several lasting relationships that continue even now. We planned and scheduled events and tried to improve upon the reputation of the church by making sure new fun things were happening there. I fought against crushing doubt and discouragement because regardless of how hard I worked and put into breathing life into that church, the altar calls I made were rarely answered and most of the time, the church fought me about anything I wanted to do. Ultimately, they fired us after almost seven years of turbulent ministry."

This part of the story was met with a moment of silence, as if the air had been sucked out of the room. All of them knew at least one person who had abandoned the faith or had been hurt by the church. Spiritual pain is difficult to recover from, and once a person is hurt by the church, they most likely never return. Craig and Kay still talked about their experiences at that first church. It left both of them deeply wounded for a long time, and they never really figured out how things went wrong there.

After a few moments, Craig's facial expression lightened up, and he continued. "But an interesting thing happened right after they fired us."

"In spite of the fact that I never really connected with the core people in the church, I developed an awesome peripheral ministry with people outside the church. I was working a full-time job handling my pastoral responsibilities but, at the same time, keeping counseling appointments three or four nights a week with people outside the church based purely on word of mouth! When word got out in the neighborhood that the church had fired us, a lady that lived three blocks from the church said, 'Well, if they don't want you, we do! How do you feel about teaching a Bible study in my garage?' We did 'Garage Church' for nearly three months after that! It was awesome! More people showed up hungry and attentive on lawn chairs in that garage during those three months than the nearly seven years I had at the church! I saw God's love for people who love him but, for whatever reasons, they feel unwelcome or awkward in church. Without good fellowship and solid teaching, their spiritual growth was hindered. I had another epiphany then and decided that Jesus didn't need another church…he needed a movement started within the church."

Paul continued to listen as Craig described what would turn out to be Thicker than Water Ministries. It was a faith-based community that purchased old abandoned buildings and turned them into ministry centers in their communities. Each one was unique to its own community and offered services for whatever was necessary. They had a massive volunteer staff for everything from childcare to car mechanics. Craig had developed a flexible leadership structure that was adaptable to each location and that allowed people to serve in their areas of giftedness. No one was turned away, and each location was provided a spiritual adviser with skills as a counselor that served as primary leadership. These leaders met people and found ways to plug them into the community. Craig held a leadership meeting once a month for all the advisers to pray and work together toward plugging new people in and strengthening each other. It was a perfect system. After a few years, it had become large enough to draw media attention. It was the local media whose interest had first been piqued. They had done enough stories about the ministry that a national news outlet picked up on it and had come to interview Craig about it.

CHAPTER 12
A Visit with Petey's Dad

Misty arrives at Pete's house during the late evening.

The only light on in the darkened house is the television in the living room. Pete's dad is sitting on a recliner about four feet back from the television. He is a fat, greasy man wearing a wifebeater tank top and faded blue jeans. There is a flimsy TV tray standing just in front of him, and he is hunchbacked over it, shoveling food into his gaping mouth. After a few minutes, he finishes gorging himself and sits back in the chair. There is a cooler on the floor next to the recliner. He reaches into it, grabs a cold beer, and rolls back into his niche in the recliner. Ralph Scott is an angry man. He works a hard job and he hates his life. He is disappointed with the man he has become and blames his wife's unexpected pregnancy with their son for ruining his plans. He was athletic when he was younger and wanted to play football in college. He was a strong competitor and would probably have been able to play professionally. When Tara wound up pregnant, he started working at the factory, and he is still there after all these years. He is so exhausted at the end of his work-day that all he wants to do is relax. Life does not pause when you come home tired from work though. There are bills that need to be paid and repairs that need done in the house. He is thankful to have the house to himself and has no remorse for the terrible beating he gave his wife the night before. He remembers his son jumping on him to protect her, and he smiles briefly to himself. It took a lot of guts for him to do that, and maybe the boy is going to grow up and be a man finally. He nearly beat Tara's sister senseless that morning as well when she came to pick up Pete for school. He decided not to because then Pete would have been home that day instead of at school. They are both gone now, and he settles in for a much-needed evening of solitude and relaxation.

He is so engrossed in the television that he does not hear the slight sound of the footsteps coming up behind him from the kitchen. Out of nowhere, a stunning Asian woman steps between him and the television. She has beautiful long jet-black hair and is wearing a skintight black jumpsuit. He is so stunned by her appearance that, at first, he did not notice that she was holding the cutting board and butcher knife from his own kitchen. His facial expression changes slightly when he notices those two items, and it is at this very moment that she smiles and says, "Hi…it's Ralph, right?"

In his sudden anger, Ralph searches for the right words to say to this intruder. When he finally picks the right words to say and begins to say them, panic sets in. He finds that not only is he unable to speak, but he is unable to move as well. She sees the panic register in his eyes and realizes that he has figured out he is paralyzed.

"It's called acupuncture, Ralph. You know it takes years of studying human anatomy to be able to paralyze a person harmlessly like that. One tiny little needle in the right place, and there you have it…frozen. Are you impressed?"

Ralph's panic gives way to an animal rage with this taunting whore, and he wishes that he could leap up from the chair and choke her with his bare hands. She sees the panic change to anger in his eyes and says, "Oh, I'm sorry… You can't answer me, can you?"

She moves toward him, smiling, and sets the butcher knife and cutting board on his lap. Then she picks up the dinner tray and moves it to the side of the television, out of her way. She moves slowly and gracefully, and she intentionally takes her time to build anger and expectation in her hostage. She turns back toward him and slowly reaches down to pick up the butcher knife. Once she has it, she takes a moment and stares into his eyes, drinking in his rage. She slides the blade of the knife across his shoulder. (For a moment, he thought she was going to stab it slowly into his throat.) Now the knife is resting with the handle on his shoulder, and the blade stabbed deeply into the material in the back of the recliner. After that, she takes his right hand from the arm of the recliner and places it on the cutting board, with the fingers spread out. She steps back a couple of times and then moves forward to shift the position of his fingers, as if she is trying to place them just right. (Either that or she is admiring how his hand looks on the cutting board. It is hard for him to tell, but now he is getting nervous.)

"Oh, Ralph, your mind is probably racing with a million questions right now. And as much as you would love for me to answer them for you, the fact is I am only going to answer one."

Her smile widens slightly, and she reaches forward to pull the butcher knife slowly from its place at his shoulder. She holds the knife up and seems to consider the sharpness of it in the flickering dim blue light from the television screen.

"My name is Misty, and I am your son Petey's schoolteacher… but I have a secret."

She stops looking at the blade and points it at him as if to threaten him. Her facial expression darkens slightly, and she asks, "Can you keep a secret, Ralph? She pauses then smiles again. "Oh, of course you can. You are completely paralyzed, aren't you?"

She steps back and tests to see that the console television will support her weight and then with the slightest jump, she is sitting on top of it, facing him. Huge drops of greasy sweat start rolling from the top of his head, and she sees fear in his eyes. Years of being a professional killer have put her in tune with different people's emotions when they are faced with a situation like this…so she sits and just smiles at him for a few moments to let his fear escalate. For Ralph, each second seems to be an eternity, and each second more, he begins to wonder if he is going to live through this. After a long pause, she says, "Oh yeah…the secret" She pauses again. "In certain circles, I am known as Razormist, and I am one of the most feared, respected, and sought-after professional killers in the entire world."

She stops to consider the knife again. She comments on how sharp and lightweight it is. Then she talks about how technology has produced sharper blades that are made out of weaker metals and that she prefers stronger blades that do not snap off when you stab a person. By now, Ralph's entire body is covered in a fine sheen of greasy sweat. The scent is putrid. Any buzz he might have had from the alcohol is completely gone now as well. He is scared to death and sure he is going to die——and worse, he is powerless to stop it from happening.

"Well, now that you know who I am, your next question is probably what I am going to do to you. Right?" She pauses again, but never stops smiling. "Well, *you* are going to have to answer that question yourself, fat boy!"

She stops talking for a few moments and then starts flipping the knife into the air and catching it. After a few moments, she fumbles a catch, and the blade flies toward him in a smooth arch. In that split second, Ralph is sure that he is going to die. His heart leaps in his chest…and he wishes he could close his eyes. The knife seems to fly toward him in slow motion. With an audible thunk, it sticks blade-first in the wooden cutting board on his lap, right next to his little finger. Now he just wants to die.

Misty slips down off the television slowly, takes a step forward, and pulls the knife from the cutting board. She then swiftly leaps backward and lands back on the spot atop the television she was sitting in just seconds before. She begins the flipping and catching the knife again as she continues speaking.

"I have a tough situation here, Ralph. See, this is the first time that I have allowed my secret life to cross over into the one I live out in the open. Really, I have to kill you to make sure that my secret is safe. If I do kill you…then Petey no longer has a dad. The real problem is I can't see how losing his dad is going to be a bad thing for Petey."

Now her facial expression changes, and she stops playing with the knife. Her smile disappears, and Ralph sees the cold, angry gaze of the professional killer for the first time. He will never forget that face.

"You are a useless, alcoholic, wife-beating, child-abusing, and greasy sack of wasted flesh, Ralph! Your putrid scent is sickening to me! I want to kill you so bad that I cannot stand it, but I want you to suffer—really suffer! My original thoughts were to cut one of those fingers off, stick it in your cooler, then watch you bleed to death. I am *sick* of seeing your son come to my class bruised and beaten, Ralph! I should torture you for what you have done to your family!

Misty stops for a second, regains her composure, and takes a few deep breaths. Once again, she slides down off the television and steps toward him. She reaches forward, grabs the tiny needle from its spot in the back of his neck and moves it to a slightly different spot. She leans back against the television again, and in a calm voice, she says, "Speak up, fat boy. See if you can convince me not to kill you."

Ralph has no idea what to say to this woman. He feels helpless and cannot think of one thing to say in his defense. He thinks of a million excuses for the man that he has become, but he is sure that Misty will not accept any of them. At this point, he is not sure that even he himself accepts any of them. He is scared, and in these few seconds that he has been given, he realizes that he has to say something...but what? What can he say to erase the hurt he has caused? What can he say to cover the mistakes he has made? Furthermore, what can he possibly say to this professional killer in order to convince her that he fully understands the message and purpose behind her coming here? In those few seconds, after all the thoughts that raced through his mind, he could only say one thing. "You're right, lady... I'm sorry."

A tear rolls down his cheek, and his eyes well up. He is broken now, and in a rush of clarity, he finally sees himself as how he truly is. Misty looks at him for a while, as if she is measuring whether or not she trusts what the man is saying. She has crossed a line this evening, and she has to be sure of her next move before she makes it. After a long period of reflection and consideration, she leans forward and speaks.

"You owe me, Ralph! You owe your son! You owe your wife! Most of all you owe yourself! Never forget the lesson you have learned this evening. Clean yourself up, and make things right. At some point in time, I will ask a favor of you. Until then, you had better fly straight. There will be no next time! If you dismiss this chance I have given you, you will suffer. Do you completely understand me?"

She looks into his eyes for the level of sincerity in the reply he will give to her ultimatum. His face is covered in sweat and tears, but he manages to take a deep breath to compose himself. His life is such a mess that he is overwhelmed with how to begin undoing all the chaos. He is a simple man, and this is how his life has progressed. He really does not know any other way. He is afraid that in some way he might seem to dismiss this chance and thus bring suffering that he surely does not want. Out of his confusion, he replies the best way that he can think of, "I understand, Misty, but I don't know where to start."

She takes a step toward him, picks up the cutting board, places both the board and the knife on the TV tray, and turns toward him again. She looks him over suspiciously and then reaches for the needle in his neck but pauses briefly to say, "Don't make the mistake of thinking that you are off the hook, Ralph. I am going to free you up, but if for one second, I feel like the old you is resurfacing, I'll cancel you clean and quick."

She pulls the needle from his neck and steps back to see what he will do next, but she is sure that he is no longer a threat. She can see in his eyes that he has been broken. Ralph stretches out in his chair a little, just enough to be sure that he can move everything again but not enough to alarm this killer in his living room. Misty crosses her arms over her chest and gives Ralph a little time to settle back into his chair. Once she is sure he is ready to listen, she hops back up onto the television and says, "Make an appointment with Pastor Craig. I will write his address and phone number down for you. Go see your wife at the hospital, take her some flowers, and apologize to her. Go pick up your son at his aunt's house, apologize to her and him, and then take your son out to eat and to see a movie. In a few days, call Craig and tell him you need help with your anger and addiction to alcohol. He is a good man, and I trust him to help you with your problems. You can mention my name to Craig, but *do not* tell him about this evening! Do not forget that you owe me, Ralph, but you are no use to me right now. Clean up your act and make things right. I don't want Petey to know about this either, so make sure you put on a good act at the next parent-teacher conference, got it?"

Ralph nods in affirmation that he understands everything that she has said. The two sit there for a moment in silence, then Misty says, "I'll show myself out."

She is distracted as she heads back to her apartment. She believes that Ralph will do what she suggested. But this was very sloppy. She cannot let her emotions get the best of her again. Her mind was racing though. In spite of how bad this lapse in judgment was, a small part of her felt good about what she had done for Petey. The thought of using her particular skill set in this way had never occurred to her.

CHAPTER 13
The Curse of Technology

The curse of technology is that nearly every human being has an electronic eye tuned in on them every day. We have become so accustomed to it that most of the time we are unaware that we are being watched. Through this eye, two different men, in two entirely different locations, watching two different televisions, point to the screen and say, "That's her!"

Miller was released from the hospital the day after his encounter with Misty. What followed was an excruciatingly long period of investigation into his private security firm. He lost seven employees that day by Misty's hand. It had been several months later, and he had not gained any new clients once word had gotten out concerning his company's catastrophic failure on that day. He had exhausted all the leads he had in trying to learn this mysterious killer's identity. He had to file bankruptcy on the company because of the settlements he had to pay out to his employees' families as a result of that day's losses. His anger had subsided and gave way to a dull throb of hatred that would only be quenched when he found this woman and ended her life the way she had so swiftly ended his. He still had his military pension to draw from, but he had grown accustomed to the lavish lifestyle that the profits from his security firm had provided. Now he was cramped in a one-bedroom studio apartment, and his life was consumed with finding her.

Miller had a successful military career. He was a decorated Marine and earned a couple of medals as a result of his time in Special Forces. He was a hard and disciplined man, but when it came time to return to civilian life, he had a difficult time adjusting. He turned to drinking shortly after his return home and got lost in the bottom of a bottle for nearly five years. One day he woke up, looked in the mirror, and just decided he had enough. He dumped whatever remaining bottles he had left and checked into a rehab center. With the help of the discipline he had learned as a Marine and six months of rehab, he kicked the habit and never took another drink. He turned his focus toward building the security firm. After over ten years of sobriety and a rocky start to the business, he was earning six figures a year and had built a strong and prosperous private security firm. His friends would tell you that he credited that firm and the creation of it as the sole purpose for maintaining his sobriety. Having to close the doors was devastating for him, and although he still had not returned to drinking, his addictive traits manifested instead as a maddening desire to find the woman who had cost him everything.

His studio apartment became his base of operations. He slept on the couch in his living room. When he woke up in the morning, he would take the time to fold up his sheets and blankets and set them at one end. He had a timer set on his coffee maker and woke up religiously every day at 6:00 a.m., right as the coffee maker started up. He ate two pieces of buttered toast and drank his first cup of coffee over the morning news and then took his second cup into the bedroom to work. There was a small desk and chair in the bedroom on the wall opposite of the door. On the center of the wall just above the desk was a picture of Misty. It was a fuzzy screen capture he had obtained from his investigations. She had disabled the cameras in the area on the day she had hit his team, and he had acquired this picture from an unrelated event that had taken place in Europe a few years prior. Spider-webbing out from that picture was a series of strings, pictures, newspaper clippings, and other items that would make any conspiracy theorist jealous. With the maps and Post-it notes he had written, the resulting web of information he had collected actually spread out to the two adjoining walls as well. What tormented him the most was that starting with the day she had taken out his team, it was as if she had disappeared completely.

He had been investigating her for months. She was like a ghost. His digging had turned up the suggestion that she was an assassin who went by the code name Razormist. The killings associated with the assassin named Razormist were the stuff of legends. She was known in certain circles all over the world as the best female professional killer the underworld had ever produced. Details were sketchy, and it was hard to sort out the gossip from what might actually be true about who she was and where she came from. Picking out stories that seemed to be generally agreed upon by several sources, he was able to put a story together concerning Razormist.

The American government frowned upon child labor, but the American military had developed a top-secret program to train a child from birth to be an assassin. Their thinking was that if you could start at an early enough age with the training, chemical enhancement would not be necessary. You could build the perfect killing machine. Their psychological studies concerning the program determined that a female child would adapt better to the training than a male child would. They also wanted to find a girl with early signs of violent tendencies and an early sense of rebelliousness. To this end, a little girl was adopted from an orphanage in mainland China. The orphanage owner, Rose, was known in the underworld for selling children via the black market. She was easily threatened by the American government toward "losing some paperwork" concerning a little Chinese girl. Miller had talked to a person off the record who had allegedly worked at the facility where the little girl was trained. This was a lucky break but turned out to be a dead end. He never found a record of the alleged orphanage or of a woman named Rose who dealt in human trafficking. If either the orphanage or Rose existed, he did not have the connections to verify the information. The confidential source that passed the information to him about the training facility would not give him an address. A call actually came to him as a warning to stop his investigation. He pried as much information that he could from the call but not enough details that he could investigate. This training facility was allegedly somewhere here in the United States, but the source would not say where.

The story picked up later when Misty was in her late teens or early twenties. She earned her name as a result of her proficiency with bladed weapons. Her trademark was her ability to leave her victims with multiple cuts and stab wounds but no apparent signs of struggle. One of the early crime scene reports stated, "It was if the victim had walked peacefully through a fine mist of razor blades and just bled out." There were several speculations throughout the files he was able to acquire concerning how she was able to do this to her victims but nothing conclusive. He had decided that if he ever was fortunate enough to find her, that she should not be underestimated. The smart thing to do would be to observe her for a while and plan an ambush.

One morning, he was enjoying his coffee and watching the news. There was a story about a groundbreaking new ministry that a young pastor had created. It had several different programs under the same roof and utilized what was once a vacant building in its neighborhood. The pastor had plans to recreate this ministry in other neighborhoods for both ministry and revitalization. Miller had no interest in the story and really only had the television on as a habit. In the background of the shot, during the interview with the pastor, two women walked into the building in the distance behind him. Miller couldn't believe his eyes. It was her—he was almost sure of it. He quickly turned up the sound and listened to the interview. The ministry was close enough to where the hit at the Clandestine happened, and that increased the possibility that it was her. It made sense. When the hit went wrong, she would have to stay somewhere nearby in order to sort out what happened. Her reputation was at stake, and she would never leave a job incomplete. Her target was Antonio Ferrante, the local mafia kingpin. He had been shaking down nearby businesses for protection money. A new adult bookstore had moved into the area, owned by a fat little Chinese man named Ting Ting. Tony, of course, ordered Ting to start paying up immediately. Tony later found out that Ting was connected to a big player in the Chinese crime syndicate. Some threats passed between Tony and the Chinese kingpin via messengers, and ultimately the kingpin hired Misty to take Tony out. It was actually by luck that

Tony found out about the price on his head. He had no idea who was coming or when, but that an attempt on his life was sure in the near future. Tony had hired a few of Miller's men as a team of bodyguards shortly after he found out about the hit being ordered.

Miller had intentionally spread some false information concerning Tony's schedule in the hopes of flushing the killer out. It worked. Tony was never supposed to be in the limousine that day. He had drastically underestimated the ferocity of the attack that day though. It was a devastating loss in so many ways. If the woman he saw in the background of this newscast was her, it was time he got some payback. He jotted down the address of the building and went to get dressed. He had to do some recon at that ministry to be sure it was her before he could plan an ambush.

*****

Julius was sitting at the bar having a drink with two of his bouncers. Encounters was the hottest club in the area, and he owned the place. It was a legitimate business, and he used it as a front for the prosperous prostitution ring he secretly ran through it. All the girls who worked for him were forced to do so after being captured, drugged, and tortured deep in the basement of this club. Over the years, he had developed a sense for the right kind of naive girls that he could exploit and pull into his secret business. He had perfected a system for breaking the girls and then using fear to keep them in line. After a year or two of working them at his club, they were usually docile and scared enough that he could relocate them under cover of night to his mansion on the outskirts of town. It was at his mansion that he entertained his more prestigious clients. Things had gone well for him for a long time, and he profited from his personal criminal empire considerably. Then one of his girls, Crystal, had somehow escaped. He had to admit, he never saw it coming. His higher paying clients found out that one of the house girls had gotten away and became nervous. The longer she was gone, the more business dropped off. His prestigious clients did not want to risk being there if she came back with the authorities. Julius was pretty sure that Crystal was scared and probably running in fear. It was not likely that she was ever coming back because ultimately that would mean having to tell people about the shameful things she had done there. That was another psychological tool he used to control his girls.

It was several months later now, and his secret business was suffering. He had ten girls when Crystal escaped. Rather than keeping them all around with no work, he was able to permanently sell seven of the girls as private slaves. He was only able to keep the two he had left working in the VIP rooms at Encounters. If it wasn't for the money he made from the club, the situation would be dire. He had a large social circle and knew several other bar owners in the area. All these were keeping an eye out for the girl and were promised a great deal of cash if they called Julius when she turned up. His higher-paying clientele were keeping the pressure on him to find her out of a sense of self-preservation. The longer she was gone, the greater the chance she could turn to the authorities for help. He could not file a missing person report with the cops, and hiring a private investigator was out of the question as well. Both would ask the kind of questions about her that he was unable to safely answer. He still had plenty of money, and the club made enough that he could live comfortably with that as his sole source of income. But the longer Crystal was gone, the more uneasy he became that investigation and legal troubles were on the horizon. Permanently selling some of the girls was both a move toward safety as well as a way to placate his higher-paying clients who were getting increasingly nervous.

If the authorities showed up, he had drastically reduced the amount of evidence they would find. The basement was cleaned out entirely now and was mainly used as storage. The training rooms he had built down there had all been dismantled, and there was no trace of them being there. The two remaining girls went home with him to the mansion when the club closed for the night or with one of the bouncers. He had five bouncers on staff, and all of them took turns taking the girls home. Any questions that might arise concerning some of the themed rooms at the mansion could be explained as personal fetishes and might be dismissed. Still, Crystal knew enough that if she talked, it would cause considerable trouble for him. He needed to find her.

The music at the club was loud, and the two televisions at each end of the bar were mostly for show. Most of the time, they were either tuned to sports or music videos. It was early in the day, so one was tuned to the local news. Encounters did not open until two in the afternoon so that the place could be cleaned and restocked each day. Business did not typically pick up until around 6:00–7:00 p.m. A few of the older patrons would come and sit at the bar for early evening drinks before the younger crowd showed up and turned the place out. The bartenders usually turned the news on for those patrons.

Julius was watching the news out of the corner of his eye. A young guy was being interviewed, but the sound was turned down, so he couldn't hear what the story was about. Suddenly, he noticed two women walking into a building in the background of the shot. He couldn't believe his eyes! It was Crystal! She had grown her hair out but was still easily recognizable.

He pointed at the television and shouted quickly to the bartender, "Turn that up!"

The story was about a ministry this young guy had built and the different ways that it had touched people's lives. He utilized an old building that had been closed for a long time and, in so doing, had revitalized that part of the neighborhood. There were plans to experiment with this same ministry in other neighborhoods. They mentioned the neighborhood a couple times in the news story, and Julius had motioned for a pad and paper to jot down where it was.

Now that he knew where to find Crystal, he could go get her and bring her back so that things could get back to normal. He pulled the two bouncers he was drinking with aside and asked them if they wanted to make some extra money that night. They were easily bought, and after Julius bought one more round for the three of them, they left the bar to go pick up his friend Crystal.

CHAPTER 14
The Painful Truth

The attack was so swift and sudden that Misty never saw it coming.

After all those months of investigation, Miller had finally caught up to the elusive killer known as Razormist. As she walked into the darkness of her apartment and he saw her from the shadows, his first thought was that she was shorter than he remembered. He held his breath and watched her head toward the light switch. He had been in the apartment a couple times before this in order to get the layout in his mind. He respected the fact that she was a professional, so he was careful to not touch anything so as not to alert her to the fact that someone had been there. The switch she was reaching for would bathe her entire living room, where he was now crouched, in a great deal of light. He had to move quickly and quietly. He knew his best chance was to catch her off guard and somehow daze her. If he could do that, he had a pretty good chance of finishing her off before she could collect herself and fight him off. Just before her finger connected with the switch, he rushed quietly up from behind her, and with the palm of his hand, he pushed her head violently into the wall just above the light switch panel.

Misty was lost in thought as she entered her apartment. Her encounter with Pete's dad was perplexing to her. She had broken the number 1 rule of the professional assassin. She had lost her cool and taken things to a personal level. Teaching this class had awakened some new feelings in her she had never experienced. The combination of that and the relationships she had begun to build at the school added up to a strange sense of peace and familiarity that she had unknowingly discovered. She had become so content in this new routine that she had briefly forgotten the person she had been beforehand. She had also attended a couple services at the church. She liked Pastor Craig and found his preaching style to be mesmerizing. For most of her life, she had never considered her own eternity or the eternity she might be sending her victims to. Now she found herself increasingly preoccupied with questions of this nature. The Bible was pretty clear that murder was a sin. She had lost count of how many murders she had been paid to commit. Surely there was no chance that God would forgive her of such a grievous amount of killing. What about her victims? Would God hold against her the fact that they might have been denied a chance to come to him had she not cancelled them out? She wanted to meet with Pastor Craig and ask him these questions, but doing so would mean having to reveal who she truly was. Over time, she had also begun to carry an unexpected amount of guilt for lying to the people around her about her secret identity.

As she reached to turn on the lights in her apartment, all these thoughts came to a screeching halt, and she was overcome with a sudden feeling, as if something were horribly wrong in this moment. It was then that her face was violently smashed into the wall above the light switch. Her head hit the wall so hard that her nose was broken and both of her eyes immediately teared up. The drywall was cracked open by the blow as her face was partially buried in it.

After smashing her face into the wall, Miller grabbed a handful of her hair and pulled her head back. He stomped his right foot down strategically on the back of her left leg, which broke her shin bone in half. Then he pulled her backward by her hair and threw her viciously to the ground. He had a knife in a leather sheath attached to his belt that he now reached for. His attack was sudden and fierce and had the desired effect of catching her entirely off guard. She was lying broken and in excruciating pain at his feet. As he paused to unsnap the sheath and grab the knife, his mind raced with all the exquisite ways that he was prepared to torture her before he finished her off. She was going to pay.

Misty was indeed in excruciating pain. It was almost unbearable. Her face was on fire, and she was nearly choking on the salty taste of blood running down the back of her throat. Nauseating waves of pain were cascading over her entire body from her left leg, which she knew was most likely broken. Time crawled at a supernaturally slow pace in these moments. She squinted in the darkness to try and clear her eyes in order to identify her assailant. She felt stupid for settling into this new life she had found and letting her guard down enough for this to happen. The guilt she had experienced for not being honest with the people around her now freshly washed over her. She was going to die in this moment, and this was going to be how those people found out who she truly was, on the nightly news. Despair overtook her momentarily, but then she realized her attacker had paused ever so briefly in his assault. In those few seconds, she reached out desperately in the only way that made sense to her and whispered quietly to herself, "Jesus, please help me."

Miller slid the knife from its sheath, but as he slid it out, it hung up on his shirt. This caused him to fumble it in his hands and drop it on the floor. His eyes were adjusted to the darkness, and he saw where it landed. In his excitement, he had stopped to look at his seemingly helpless victim. Based on all the stories he had uncovered about her in his investigation, he had expected her to be much harder to subdue even with the element of surprise he had gained. As he reached down to pick up his knife, he smiled at the good fortune of things going so easily.

Through the mind-numbing pain of this moment, Misty heard a faint thump on the ground next to her. She was looking for any way possible to gain the upper hand. In her fog of pain, she saw the silhouette of a man's face moving down toward her. In spite of the tears in her eyes, she was able to take one desperate strike in the direction of that silhouette to try and save herself.

As Miller bent down to pick up his knife, which had landed on the floor right next to Misty's head, she struck him perfectly on his jawline in a way that rendered him immediately unconscious. He slumped over sideways and landed on the floor next to her.

Misty lay there on the floor for several minutes and gained her composure. Her eyes gradually cleared and adjusted to the darkness of her apartment. The man on the floor next to her looked vaguely familiar, but she could not place him. She had no idea how long he was going to be out and decided her best chance of survival was to flee for now and regroup. The pain in her leg had settled to a dull throb, and she was sure it was broken. She needed medical attention, but she could not risk going to the hospital and being identified. With a broken leg, she could not get far on foot. She felt hopeless and alone and, at the same time, an urgency to get moving. All at once, it came to her, and she knew where she had to go. She had no idea how all this was going to work out, but she was out of options for the time being. She took a deep breath and pulled herself up to a standing position on her one good leg, took one last look at her assailant and said, "You can see yourself out."

Thankfully, she made it out to the parking lot and into her car unnoticed. The journey seemed to take a lifetime, and she nearly passed out from the pain several times. She took a few minutes to rest before she started the car. She usually used both feet when she drove, but she was able to get where she needed to be using only her unbroken leg. She took a deep breath, got out of her car, and made her way up to the door. She knew that what she was about to do was going to change everything in ways she could not anticipate, but she really had nowhere else to turn. After a considerable amount of hesitation, she rang the doorbell.

It was late in the evening. Craig and his wife had settled down in front of the television to relax for a little while before going to bed. They had both reached such a state of relaxation when the doorbell sounded that there was brief moment of nonverbal communication between them as they decided who was going to go answer the door. Kay smiled at Craig and said, "You owe me one." Craig smiled back and nodded in agreement. Kay got up and made her way to the door. When she answered it, the shock nearly knocked her over. It was Misty. She was covered in blood and leaning against the doorframe. Her eyes were so badly blackened and swollen that, for a moment, Kay did not recognize her. She turned to Craig and with a desperate exhale said, "*Oh my god!* Craig!" Based purely on the expression of his wife's face, he jumped up and raced over to the door. He was equally unprepared for how horribly beaten Misty was.

Misty said, "I'm sorry, but I had nowhere else to go."

Craig and Kay helped her into the house and shut the door. Misty told them that she thought her leg was broken, so Kay rushed into the kitchen to grab a chair for her to sit on. They helped her sit down and looked her over. After a few minutes of shocked silence, Craig looked over at Kay and then back to Misty and asked, "What happened to you?"

Once she decided to ring that doorbell, Misty simultaneously decided on a certain course of action, and now it was time to take that action. She looked at Craig and Kay with tears welling in her eyes and said, "I have not been honest with all of you concerning who I am..."

CHAPTER 15
And the Truth Shall Set You Free

"My name is Misty, but in other parts of the world, I am known as Razormist, and I make my living as a professional killer."

It was hard for her to say, but some part of her was relieved to finally be unburdened. She searched Craig and Kay's faces for what their reaction to this truth was going to be. After a few moments, Craig looked at her, then over to Kay and softly said, "The Clandestine Hotel hit." Misty was shocked by these words. How was it possible that Craig could make that connection so swiftly? Kay's eyes widened slightly, and then a warm smile came over her face. Craig had talked to her many times concerning Misty. He considered her to be a blessing for the school and the kids took to her immediately. But something had been nagging at Craig about her since the day they first met. Craig had a supernatural gift when it came to people. It was like he could see right into them. He could not put a finger on it, but Kay had lived with him long enough that she knew if Craig had a sense about Misty, then there was something to it. She was not shocked at all to see him make the connection so quickly, and something inside her sensed immediately that he was right. Misty was exhausted by now and a little confused by their nonverbal communication at the moment. She simply replied, "Yes...that was me."

The silence hung over the three of them like a magic spell for a few moments, but it popped like a bubble when Craig finally spoke up. "Well, we can talk about that later. Are you still bleeding?"

Kay loved Craig. He was a man of action. For many years his heart had burned for the ministry they had founded. She never grew tired of his ability to adapt to whatever challenges they had faced. Over the years, she had watched him push through doubt and anger as Christ gradually built the ministry he had always known in his heart was possible. This ministry touched the hearts of people from all walks of life. Craig had a God-given gift for finding ways to plug people into the ministry, and over the years, it turned out to be a great community of believers that seemed more like a lovingly tight-knit family. Misty was sitting here, bleeding all over their kitchen chair. She had just admitted to them that she was an assassin and that she was responsible for at least ten deaths in the not so distant past. Craig, however, looked right past that to the immediate need she had for medical attention. She loved him for that.

"My nose is broken. That is where the blood came from. I am pretty sure my left shin is broken. As far as I know, besides a few bumps and bruises, those are my primary injuries. Obviously, I cannot go to the hospital. I don't even know why I came here. I got lucky and got away, and it just made sense in the moment."

"You're fine," Craig said. "So how does the other guy look? Do we need to call a squad or the coroner?"

Misty managed a slight chuckle. "Neither for now. I was able to knock him out and get away before he snapped out of it. He attacked me in my apartment. He will be long gone before anybody could get there to investigate."

Kay asked, "Is there any chance that this guy followed you here?" Misty reassured Kay that the chance of that was very slim. Even if he did regain consciousness before she pulled out of the lot and saw what direction she left in, he could not have known exactly where she was going. Craig had settled down a little now that he knew Misty's injuries were not as terrible as they looked. He asked her if she knew the guy who attacked her. She had also calmed down considerably by now and as she was relaying the story to them had remembered an important detail she had forgotten. A strange kind of warm shock fell over her in that moment as she came to that point in the story.

"Oh my god! The knife…on the floor…"

All at once she remembered that moment and realized what had happened. Her eyes once again welled up with tears. Was it possible that he heard her? Was it possible in that moment that he had stretched out his hand to protect her? Could three small words really have released that much power? Craig and Kay looked curiously at her and waited for an explanation of that last statement. The tears started streaming down her face as she remembered those three words: "Jesus, help me."

Through her tears, Misty relayed to them what happened. "He caught me completely off guard. I was lying at his feet in excruciating pain waiting for him to finish me off. I remember wondering in the moment what he was waiting for. I heard a thump on the carpet next to my head. I blew it off at the time. I saw him leaning down toward me and just managed to knock him out in the dark with a lucky shot. I noticed the knife on the floor when I left. While I was lying there, desperate and hopeless, I asked Jesus to help me. He must have dropped his knife on the floor next to me in that moment and reached down to pick it up. That is why he bent down, and that's how I was able to take that shot at him."

Misty had a distant look in her eyes as she spoke now, as if she were lost in thought. She asked Kay and Craig, "Is that stupid? Does God work like that?"

Now it was Kay and Craig's turn to well up with tears. Every once in a while, God did something wonderful for a person that the untrained eye would totally miss. God saved Misty's life tonight. But he did more than that. He showed himself to her in a way that made sense to her in the context of her life. He desires to do this for everyone, but too many Christian people are conditioned by human tradition to not see God's work in this way. Over the years, Craig and Kay had seen God work personally like this in their own lives, as well as in the lives of many people around them. They never underestimated what God would do to show himself to someone. Now there was a professional killer in their living room who had apparently just escaped death because of God's intervention. Ignoring the blood now drying on Misty's shirt, Kay walked over to her, hugged her, and said, "Yes, he does, Misty. Yes, he does."

Craig left the two of them to talk and said, "I need to go make some calls."

As the ministry progressed, Craig had found a need to befriend a few doctors. There were always prostitutes who escaped a pimp who was beating them or gang members who were looking for a way out after receiving a gunshot wound. These kinds of people need medical attention but cannot typically rely on their insurance plan at work. He had said in mixed company from time to time that it was important to have a "good doctor friend that you can call at two in the morning when something extreme happens." Tonight, his professional killer friend needed some medical attention and, probably, a cast on her leg. The first call he made was to Phillip Robbins. Dr. Robbins was formerly an Army medic and had a modest family practice in a nearby town. He was an older man and sort of a rugged type. He liked to poke fun at Craig's youth, but he was impressed by how much Craig had accomplished in ministry for how young he was. He actually had contacted Craig personally to offer his services several years ago after having heard about the ministry from a mutual friend. Craig had taken him out to lunch several times since then, and the two were pretty good friends. Phil was also a believer and had an uncommon heart for ministry that made him the perfect person to call for this particular situation. It was around midnight when he called, and luckily Phil was still up.

"Craig? Isn't it past your bedtime, young man?"

Craig chuckled slightly and began with "You are not going to believe this…" He relayed the events of the night to Phil. Phil listened intently to the story and asked a few questions of his own to determine what supplies he might need to pick up at his office before he came to the house. Phil decided it might be less painful for Misty if he treated her at Craig's house, plus they might draw some unwanted attention if he had opened up his office at this late hour. Kay and Craig had a spare room they could let Misty use for a while during the healing process, but they had some guest speakers lined up in a few weeks that would need the room. Now that Phil was on the way, he took some time to pray and seek guidance from God concerning how to move forward. Many times, he had found himself in outlandish situations as a result of the ministry and its challenges, but this was a first. He was certain that God had sent Misty, and now that he knew the truth about her that had been nagging him for some time, it was time to seek God and find out what part he was supposed to play.

When he finally came out of his study and rejoined the ladies, they were both sitting in the living room on the couch and sipping some hot tea. Loki was lying on the couch next to Misty and was totally oblivious to the fact that she was a killer. All he cared about was the slow rhythmic scratching he was getting on his head, which was currently pushing him deeply into his late evening nap. Kay had helped Misty get cleaned up and made an ice pack for her nose. She had helped Misty get out of her bloody clothes and gave her a top and some shorts. Kay had a larger build than Misty, but her clothes were not too large on her to be awkward. A nasty black-and-purple bruise had formed on Misty's leg, and you could see a large bump just under the skin that would not ordinarily be there. The bone was definitely broken. Kay and Craig had an uncanny ability to have entire conversations with each other at a glance. They caught eye contact with each other when he walked in the room and saw the bruise on Misty's leg. He knew they were both thinking the same thing. How can she just sit there and sip hot tea and not curl up in a ball as a result of those injuries. Misty's indifference to the pain seemed to verify that she was who she claimed to be.

Craig told Misty that he had a doctor friend, and that he was on the way to the house to treat her injuries. Kay asked him, "Is Dr. Phil coming over?" They shared a brief chuckle about that. Phil was nothing like the television personality in looks or behavior, and because of the lighthearted teasing they both took from him about their youth, they enjoyed calling him that. Craig smiled and affirmed that Phil was who he had called.

After that, he sat down in his chair across from Misty to have a chat with her before Phil arrived. There were still some details that needed sorted out, but some immediate action needed to be taken. It was this plan that he needed to establish with Misty. He started the conversation.

"Okay, your secret is safe with us for now. You have heard me teach that people are responsible for their actions. I will agree to help you if you will agree to take responsibility for your actions. I am no use to the people who rely on me in this ministry if I go to jail for harboring a fugitive. Get your stuff sorted out." Misty nodded her approval.

Craig continued, "My friend Phil is a good doctor and was a medic in the Army when he was younger. I trust him, and you can too. I told him who you are and how you were injured. He was also moved by the fact that God intervened for you tonight and is thankful for the opportunity to come and patch you up. He is the only person we will tell your secret to. If you tell anyone else, that is up to you. You are welcome to stay here and recover for a couple weeks, but we have some guests coming, and they will need the room. I have prayerfully considered a few friends through the church who might put you up for the rest of your recovery secretly. Give me some time, and I will set it up. I will tell the staff at the school that you had to go out of town for a family emergency to buy you some time to recover. I am sure you can develop your own backstory to tell them when you come back." Craig added a slight touch of lighthearted sarcasm to that last statement. Misty thanked Craig and Kay for everything, and in her heart, she knew she had come to the right place.

The three of them sipped tea and sat quietly, waiting for the doctor to arrive. It was going to be a long night, but each of them had a sense that God was doing something amazing in their midst, and each one had an entirely different expectation for what that might be.

CHAPTER 16
Best Friends Forever

The primary qualification for being best friends is the ability to keep each other's secrets.

Crystal did not really trust Misty at the beginning. When Pastor Craig pulled her aside and asked if Crystal was willing to let her move in and keep it a secret, it made her uneasy. Craig and his wife had done so much to help her though that she kind of felt obligated to do it. All she knew was that Misty had been attacked and hurt pretty badly and that she could not go back to her own place until either she healed or until the cops figured out who had done it. Craig and his staff did an excellent job of helping people without asking questions, and she admired that about them. Although she had been living here for a few months, she still was uneasy that Julius might find her, and for that reason, she was perpetually cautious. Letting Misty move in without knowing who it was that attacked her or why the attack had taken place was unsettling to her. She had already decided after Craig had come by to drop her off that she was going to ask some questions.

She knew Misty. There was a huge buzz about the school the first day she had come on as a teacher. The rumor was that Craig had met her at the gym. She was absolutely gorgeous, and all the females were typically catty behind her back out of jealousy the first couple weeks she was there. She was soft-spoken and kind. It was not too long before the staff and the kids took to her and she fit right in. Something didn't settle with Crystal though. Misty just seemed too perfect to her. She had no concrete reason to distrust her, but over the years, she had developed an instinct when it came to people. Crystal was sure there was something Misty was hiding, but she kept it to herself. She had remembered a quote from the Bible one time that said something about the eyes being the window to the soul. For the most part, she had found that to be true. Most people do not make eye contact when they speak. They will look briefly at you, but their eyes shift to either look you over or look behind you. Crystal had noticed that Misty locked eyes with you when she spoke to you. Her smile was disarming, and most people would not notice because of their own wandering eyes. Crystal only had a handful of brief conversations with Misty, but they each carried a strange mutual sense of evaluation as long as they lasted. She had been home from work at the cafeteria for a couple of hours when the doorbell rang. She took a deep breath and whispered a quick prayer as she went to answer the door.

Crystal was shocked at first when she opened the door. Misty was worse than she had expected. Her face was bruised and cut up pretty bad. One of her legs was in a cast from the ankle all the way up to the top of her thigh. Craig had an arm around her and appeared to be supporting most of her weight. Crystal stepped aside and motioned toward her couch for Craig to set Misty there. Misty had to be in pain, but it did not register on her face. She smiled at Crystal as Craig placed her on the couch and thanked her for opening her home to her. In the moment, she noticed that in spite of her condition, she had never broke eye contact with Crystal from the moment she opened the door. Once Misty was settled and Crystal closed the door, Craig took some time to brief Crystal on the situation.

"Thank you for helping me out on this one. I know it was a lot to ask, and I'm sorry for asking in the way I did. Trust me when I say I am feeling my own way through this one, and I wish I could tell you more. We are telling the people at the school that Misty had a family emergency and that she had to leave town unexpectedly. Your place is far enough away that I don't think anyone will see her here. I am prayerfully considering a couple other people to watch over her until she heals up, so I am thinking I only need her here for a couple weeks at the most… I hope that will be okay?"

Crystal replied, "I trust you, Pastor, and I would not do this for anyone but you and Kay. You guys have been wonderful to me, and I am glad to help out. I will not lie though—I am a little uncomfortable with this. Are there any special instructions I need to help take care of her?"

Misty replied to this one herself, "I am just weak for now. I just need a place to crash basically until my leg heals. More importantly, I just need to be in a place where I can heal without worrying about these creeps coming back to finish the job."

Craig briefly hugged both ladies and said, "Okay, you two will be fine. I have a million things to do before bedtime, so I will leave you two to sort things out. Have a good night." With that, he turned and let himself out. There was a bit of an awkward silence between the two after he left because neither one knew what to do next. Misty hated being in such a vulnerable state and was angry at herself still for being caught slipping. She had settled into this life and let her guard down enough that her life was in danger. Crystal was uneasy due to all the questions she had about Misty, and she just wasn't sure what the next step should be. Crystal said, "Well, let me slip into my night clothes, and then we can figure out something to eat."

Crystal prepared a meal and some hot tea, and the two sat next to each other and ate dinner in silence. Misty was lost in thought, and Crystal just didn't know what she wanted to say first. It was Misty who wound up breaking the silence, and Crystal was totally unprepared for what Misty had to say.

Misty had been thinking about all this since Craig had opened the door and dragged her into his house nearly dead. She had developed a love for these people. She didn't want any of them to get hurt. In her current condition, she was unable to fight or protect them if the worst should happen. She had told Craig the truth about who she was, and she had to admit that she was shocked at how easily he took the news. For just being a pastor, she was surprised at the connections he had and how quickly he was able to spirit her away and help her find the help she needed. When he called upon people to help, they did so immediately and without question. He was a good man, and it was humility that was his greatest characteristic in her opinion. It was the thing about him that most people responded to. He loved people, and he reached out to everyone. Once you knew him, you were grateful to come along with him and help the others he was reaching out to because he had reached out to you the same way. Everyone she had met since coming on to teach at Thicker Than Water Academy exhibited his characteristic servanthood. She loved that, and she was determined to heal as fast as possible so she could deal with this situation before any of these wonderful people got hurt.

She had talked with this Crystal on a handful of occasions and could tell she had a history that most people might not pick up on. Most people do not look you in the eye when they talk to you, but Crystal always held eye contact when she spoke to her. She sensed that Crystal was reading her, but not in a challenging way. It was necessary for her to be vague and secretive as much as possible with these people, but she sensed that Crystal might be a person she could befriend if things had been different. Now she was beaten badly and unable to fight for the time being. She had no idea how long she would be here with Crystal, and honestly, she wasn't sure how long she could tolerate the awkward silence. In the moment, she decided to take a risk and reach out to Crystal. They had finished dinner, and Crystal had taken the dishes into the kitchen to wash them. She returned with a fresh cup of tea for both of them and sat down once again beside her on the couch. She had a look in her eye as if she had something to say.

Misty started the conversation. "I really appreciate you opening your place to me. I know you have a lot of questions, and as it is, I have nothing but time, so…ask them."

Crystal wasn't prepared for things to be that easy, but she was relieved that it worked out that way. She had been rehearsing how to start the conversation in her mind all evening. She didn't want to be nosy, but at the same time, she could not keep from needing to know some answers. She would not have been able to rest in her own home without them as long as this person was staying with her.

Crystal began, "Who did this to you, and why did they do it?"

Misty answered, "I am prepared to tell you everything, but I need to know that you can keep this secret. A lot of people can get hurt if you don't."

Crystal carried her own closet full of secrets and was pretty sure that whatever Misty was getting ready to tell her could not be nearly as bad as any of that. She replied, "I've kept some secrets of my own. I know how to keep yours."

Misty appreciated Crystal's bluntness, so she started in on her story. "You all know me as Misty, but in other circles, I am known as Razormist. I am a freelance professional killer. I moved into this area several months ago to kill a man, but the job went wrong. Someone found out where I live and sent men to kill me there, but I managed to escape to Pastor Craig's house and get away from them. Right now, I cannot be sure who came after me or why. It could either be guys from the person who hired me or from the person I was hired to kill. I have been doing this for a long time, and to be honest, this is the first time I have been in a situation like this. As soon as I can get back on my feet, I intend to go find whoever did this to me and cancel them out clean and quickly."

Her words hung in the air for a short time. Crystal was not sure at first if this could be true. Misty had spoken them so firmly though that it was impossible she could be lying. Crystal suddenly remembered the failed attempt on Anthony Ferranti's life in the news, and all at once, things fell into place. Sitting here, on the couch with her, was the woman that police had been searching for in connection with that attempted murder. She fought to catch her breath. She was immediately fascinated with this woman and wanted to know everything she could about her. She had always felt there was something hidden about her, but this was huge. She had seen movies about such things but never considered that real people actually did them. She also realized the importance of this moment. This was an unprecedented act of trust on Misty's behalf. People really could be in danger if this secret got out. In a weird way, Crystal had kind of been made a partner with Misty now in all this. There was so much Crystal wanted to know now, yet she was completely unable to figure out what to ask next. As all these thoughts spun around in her mind, she uttered, "Oh my god…in the news…it was you?"

Misty collected her thoughts for the moment. She had opened up to this young woman. It was too late to back out now. She could laugh, play it off like she was joking, and make up a different story concerning what happened. But it honestly felt good to her in the moment to reach out to someone and release this truth. She had decided to reach out to Crystal, and there was no point in turning back now. So she pushed forward and she answered Crystal's question, "Yes, it was. I have been working to figure out what happened. It turned out that I needed to stay here longer than expected. When I met Craig at the gym and he offered me this job, it worked out to be the perfect cover for me until I can get to the bottom of this."

Crystal asked more questions about the job Misty had come to do. Why was the hit ordered on this man's life? What went wrong, and when did she figure out that something wasn't right? How long had Misty been doing this job? Where did she train? What places had she traveled to in the world? Crystal's enthusiasm was uncontainable, and Misty could not help but smile and entertain her with more answers. It was unexpectedly nice to just share her life with this person. She didn't really realize until this moment how lonely her existence had been.

After Misty had shared for a long time, she looked to Crystal and said, "So enough about me, how did you end up here?"

Crystal's face went blank for a moment, and her eyes glazed over as if she suddenly went into a state of deep thought. She felt a connection now with Misty like no one she had ever know before. She replied, "Let me go make some more tea, and I will tell you my story." She got up and took both cups to the kitchen.

Misty had drunk so many cups of tea that nature took effect on her. She asked Crystal to help her to the restroom to relieve herself. Crystal was not as strong as Craig, and Misty was a lot heavier than she expected. Misty had a real sense of urgency, and Crystal was trying really hard to get her there quickly. At one point, they both fell in the hallway on the way. Misty gasped in pain, and Crystal immediately said, "Oh my god, I'm sorry… I'm sorry… Oh my god!"

The sheer helplessness they both experienced in the moment caused them both to bust out laughing. They managed to get the job done together though and somehow to get Misty back to the couch, but now laughing uncontrollably the whole time. Crystal helped Misty get changed into some more comfortable clothes for bed and spread a sheet over the couch for Misty to sleep on. She found a spare pillow and blanket as well and set them on the floor, next to the couch, for when Misty was ready to retire. Crystal warmed the two cups of tea that had cooled off by then and began her story for Misty.

"My dad was a Baptist minister. He raised us in a strictly religious home. We traveled and sang as a family for a long time. I was always different on the inside. My dad and I fought a lot, and I always felt that he loved my sisters more than me. By the time I was eighteen years old, I was more than ready to move out on my own. I had a great apartment with two older girls I had met. There was this club I really wanted to go to with them called Encounters. I took the day off on my twenty-first birthday and spent it getting ready to finally go there. I barely remember the inside of the place now..."

Crystal trailed off for a moment, and tears welled up in her eyes as she began the tale of what happened to her and all the things she endured up until she met Pastor Craig. Misty had to dry her own eyes a couple times as Crystal shared the painful story of her life. She felt a deep connection to this young woman, and although it was forged in a different way, she admired the strength she had developed which in many ways was not all that different from her own. She felt a lot of things in this moment, but above them all were intense desires to find this man Julius and make him suffer—really suffer.

The two were up talking until early in the morning of the next day, and in that time, a strong and lasting friendship took root. Misty continued to heal, and Crystal kept her secretly hidden away to allow her to do so.

*****

Several weeks had passed, and other than the cast on her leg, Misty had fully healed from that night's injuries. She was able to get herself up and around the apartment, and even took to cooking dinner for Crystal before she got home from work. Craig had prayerfully sought out another place for her to finish out her recovery and had come to the conclusion that his friends Paul and Julianna were the ones to call upon for that favor. He had already called them, and of course, they had agreed. An additional benefit to Misty finishing her recovery there was that Paul had a decent gym set up in his basement that she could have daily access to in order to build her strength back up. Julianna was dying of cancer, and in exchange for moving in, she was to aid Paul in caring for her as she lived out the rest of her days here on earth.

This was to be the last night Misty stayed at Crystal's apartment. It was actually supposed to be a night sooner, but a sudden scheduling conflict had bumped the date a night forward.

When Crystal got home, Misty had dinner prepared, and the two had a couple glasses of wine with dinner before settling on the couch for the evening to talk. They had become good friends over the past few weeks, and both had decided they were going to miss each other's constant company. Neither of them had ever met Paul and Julianna, but they knew the majority of the financing for the ministry as a whole came from that couple. Julianna's cancer had come upon her swiftly, and most of the people at Thicker Than Water were shocked by the news. It was a beautiful story how the two of them came together, which in a way added a deeper note of sadness to the news.

It was late in the evening on that last night when the doorbell to Crystal's apartment rang. The ladies were at peace and had laughed and enjoyed each other's company all evening. Crystal rarely had someone at the door aside from the occasional salesperson or Jehovah's Witness. Still, there was no cause for alarm. Crystal smiled at Misty and jokingly said, "Don't get up, I'll get that." Misty laughed lightly and said, "Gee, thanks." Crystal unlocked the door and began to pull it open enough to see who it was when the door was violently shoved open from the outside. Crystal fell back a few feet away from the door, and two very large men forced their way into the apartment, with another smaller man walking in lightly behind them.

The first two men were over six feet tall and about three hundred pounds each by Misty's estimation. They were both gruff biker-looking types, and Misty figured they were more brutish fighters who were used to having a weight advantage over their opponents. Crystal looked past the two bigger men, and with tears forming in her eyes, she said, "Julius?"

Julius shut the door behind him and looked at Crystal lying on the floor. He smiled at her and said, "My favorite girl. Lisa, how have you been, baby?"

One of the biker guys looked over at Misty sitting on the couch. Her face lit up with a huge and still-growing smile.

"Look, boss, we got two for the price of one."

The other brute said, "Oh, I'll take the Asian one on the couch. She looks hot."

Crystal was overcome with fear at first. Her worst nightmares had finally come true, and Julius was here to drag her back to the horrible life that she had once escaped. Somehow, in that moment, a thought came to her mind. Gradually, her fear faded as she realized what was about to unfold right here in her apartment. She had recently acquired a new best friend. This best friend was a highly skilled, internationally known professional killer. She was sitting on the couch in her apartment right now. She looked over at the couch as she began to get up from the floor to see that Misty had repositioned herself to the center of the couch and was patting both seats next to her motioning for the biker type guys to sit with her.

In a low, sexy voice, Misty said, "Who are your friends, Lisa? Come here and sit with me, boys."

Both bikers blushed and looked toward their boss for approval to do what both of them wanted desperately and eagerly to do, sit with Misty. He nodded in their direction and said, "Be gentle with her for now, boys, while I take care of my business." They sat with Misty and leaned in close to her.

She put her arms up on the back of the couch as if to hug them as they sat down. *Stupid, brutish thugs,* she thought.

The moment they were in the right position for her to do so, she firmly pressed the sharp end of the buttons she had pulled off the couch into the perfect pressure points on the backs of their necks. They were both instantly paralyzed, motionless and helpless with their fat, stupid grins.

Misty's action was so seamless that from Julius's perspective his two bodyguards had merely sat down and were watching him to see what the next move was with smiles of contentment on their fat faces. Crystal had no idea that the two big guys were already dealt with, but a sudden rage came over her. She looked over at Misty and realized that she was using her eyes to subtly suggest something to her. She motioned toward the wine bottle sitting on the table in front of her, but there was another movement she was suggesting that she could not figure out. She controlled her rage and instinctively moved in a way that put Julius between them so that he could not see the eye contact between them. Julius began to speak in a low but angry tone, totally unaware of what was about to happen…

"Do you have any idea how much money you have cost me? Do you know how much money and effort I had to put into finding you? You have a long list of clients who were very upset when you took off. They were so worried that you would turn them in that I had to assure them I would find you and bring you quickly back to them. Once word got out that one of my girls escaped, of course, most of my other clients stopped coming as well. This little adventure of yours is over, and *if* you live through what I am about to do to you, you are getting right back to work earning back every penny by yourself!" After saying this, he moved toward Crystal, prepared to subject her to the worst beating he had ever exacted upon anyone. Unfortunately, in his rage and excitement over finding Crystal, he neglected a very important detail. He should have taken the time to ask who the beautiful Asian woman was seated on her couch.

In one moment, he was reaching to grab Crystal, and in the next, a very heavy wine bottle shattered in a million pieces right at the base of his skull, knocking him out face-first onto the living room carpet. Crystal was so close to him that when the bottle exploded on the back of his head, not a single drop of the spray reached her. The wall behind her was covered in almost a perfect outline of her shape.

She saw Misty pick the bottle up and saw her throw it. When it hit, she simply stepped aside and let Julius' limp form drop to the floor.

A rush of emotions came over Crystal. She wasn't sure if she should be ecstatically happy or horribly terrified. Misty leaned forward and got up from the couch. She looked at the two biker guys and said, "Sit tight, boys... I'll be right back." It was then that Crystal realized both of them were helplessly paralyzed on the couch. Tears welled up in her eyes, but for some reason, great bellows of hysterical laughter issued from her mouth. In mere moments, three very dangerous men were completely subdued, silently, and without any real mess or scuffle. Misty walked over to Crystal, hugged her, and asked her if she was okay. Crystal, still laughing with tears in her eyes, said, "Oh my *god*! That was *awesome*!"

Misty just smiled flatly. She had flipped that switch inside her mind and had now entered into professional killer mode. She looked Crystal in the eye and said, "Get yourself together, girl, then do me a favor and go to the kitchen and grab your sharpest butcher knife for me—and some paper towels to clean up some of this mess."

Crystal had never seen Misty like this, and it was easy for her to forget how dangerous her newly acquired friend was because prior to tonight, it was not reality for her. Seeing Misty like this silenced her laughter, and she quickly went to get the items Misty had requested. They cleaned the splatters of wine from the wall and then cleaned up the back of Julius head as best as they could. Crystal helped Misty lean Julius's limp form up against the wall and placed a thumbtack in his sweet spot as well to paralyze him in the same manner as the other two guys. Once this was accomplished, Crystal asked Misty what to do next. Misty answered, "Now we wait for lover boy here to wake up and see to it that he and his pals never bother you again." Crystal hugged Misty tightly and thanked her again and again for this. She could hardly deal with the possibility that her running might actually be over forever. Misty on the other hand had no doubt that her newly acquired friend was never going to have to run from this problem ever again.

It was about thirty minutes before "lover boy" woke up. Panic registered in his eyes as he realized that he and his pals were helpless.

Crystal looked to Misty when she noticed Julius had awakened, and Misty just smiled and said to her, "Do you want to help…or do you want me to just take care of it?" Crystal had no idea what to do with this situation, so she replied, "You're the professional… I think I'll just sit back and watch you work." With this, Misty grabbed the butcher knife from the coffee table, smiled at Julius widely, and walked around the table to sit once again between the two biker bodyguards. She took a moment to look really close in each of their eyes. Both were sweating, stiff, and terrified by now, waiting to see what was going to happen to them.

Misty slowly straddled the first one, took the butcher knife, and carved a small but deep R in the center of his chest. Tears streamed down his hopeless face, and his breath escalated, but all he could do was sit there helplessly. She pressed a paper towel against the wound and then slowly and patiently maneuvered herself over to the other biker. She straddled him and carved the same small but deep R on his chest. Great tears streamed down both their faces, and Crystal was uneasy at this point. She was slightly scared, but at the same time, she trusted that her friend knew what she was doing. Overall, she was tired of running, and the possibility that this was all going to be over when Misty was finished kept her entranced as she watched her friend work.

Misty pressed a paper towel over the second biker's wound then slowly spun off his lap and back to sitting on the couch between them. She stared angrily into Julius's eyes and let him ponder what was going to happen to him while at the same time watching the bloody spot grow on the paper towel on his bodyguards' chests. After a short time, Misty pushed herself off the couch and crossed the room to get right down in Julius's face. With her leg in the cast, it took a little maneuvering to do so, and Crystal wasn't sure whether or not Misty took this extra time for added effect. Misty slowly unbuttoned Julius' shirt and then carved a slightly larger and slightly deeper R on his chest. She buttoned his shirt closed and then pressed it tightly against his bleeding wound. She handed the knife to Crystal and told her to clean it thoroughly then throw it in the trash. While Crystal did that, Misty got herself up from the floor and stood in a place where she could stare angrily into the eyes of all three men.

When Crystal came back into the room, Misty addressed all three men openly. "I have marked all three of you now… You are *my* hookers. From now on, your name is Lisa. I do not care what your name was before now…it does not exist. If you use that old name and I find out, I will kill you in a way that your little pansy heart could never imagine. *This* is my friend Crystal. Whatever business you had with her is my business now, and it does not exist. If she ever sees you again or any unnatural harm ever comes to her, I will kill you and your parents in ways that your little pansy hearts could never imagine. The only reason I am letting you live is because this stupid cast on my leg would make it too difficult to dispose of your bodies. So consider this your lucky day."

Then Misty walked over to Julius. She bends down as close to his face as the cast on her leg will allow her to and says, "When I get this cast removed, I might still come and kill you anyway. Use this as a golden opportunity from God to change your profession. Thank him every day that he made it inconvenient for me to kill you right now, and beg him every day that I don't find you and kill you later. It is taking every fiber of my being to not gut you right now. Remember that!"

Misty stepped away from Julius and said to all three men, "I am going to let you go one at a time. Walk out quietly, one at a time… and keep walking. When I am satisfied that one is far enough away, I will let the next one go. I will tell you now that if you're entertaining the idea of gathering outside and storming back in here for revenge, *please* do it. I want to kill you so bad I can taste it."

With that, she stood by the door and had Crystal release the first biker from the couch. As he exited the apartment, she looked him in the eye and smiled, spanked him lightly, and said, "Have a good night… Lisa." He just kept his head down and walked out quietly, happy to be escaping this ordeal with his life. Misty waited a few minutes and then signaled for Crystal to let the second biker go free. He too was humiliated as he was let go, and he too walked out without incident, happy to still be alive. Neither man waited for Julius to be released. They met up down the road and walked away to leave him to whatever his fate was. Julius never saw either of them again.

When it was just Crystal, Misty, and Julius left in the apartment, Misty asked Crystal a question. "Here is the man you have been running from. Can you live out the rest of your life peacefully, trusting that he will never bother you again?"

Crystal had to ponder this for a few minutes. She could not bring herself to believe that her ordeal quite possibly had come to such an abrupt end. Julius was a ruthless man. Could she really believe his life had been changed by this encounter? She looked into his seemingly helpless eyes for some clue toward whether or not she could let him go free and still feel safe. She asked Misty, "What can we do if I say no?"

Without hesitation, and as if she had already considered how to answer this question, Misty flatly replied, "Then it will be a long night. We will get that butcher knife back out of the trash, cut him into small pieces all night, and flush him down the toilet one piece at a time. The only additional things we would need are some trash bags and those dish gloves under the kitchen sink. He is helpless, and we could just transfer him to the tub. Whatever is left when we are done, we can just simply clean out of the tub. That might have been an impossible task with his pals, but he is probably only 175 pounds, I think we could finish him before you have to work in the morning. It really doesn't matter to me." She smiled at Julius and added, "Honestly, if it was up to me, he would already be in the tub and his fingers and toes would have already had their burial at sea."

She couldn't explain why, but the flatness with which that last statement had been uttered by Misty caused Crystal to laugh out loud. In that moment, Misty saw the weight that had been crushing her friend the whole time she had known her lift from her shoulders and her heart. They laughed together for a few moments with Julius staring blankly at them from the floor. This struck both of them even funnier, and they laughed a little harder. Crystal got down in Julius's face and asked him, "What do you think about a burial at sea, Captain Ahab?" Misty chuckled and said under her breath, "Thar she blows." At that, they both burst out laughing with tears in their eyes. It took a few moments for them to calm back down.

As much as she hated Julius and as bad as she knew he was, Crystal had decided she could not live with herself knowing she had literally flushed a man down the toilet one piece at a time. She had been turning this choice over in her mind and was also pretty confident that Misty had generated enough fear in him to leave her alone. She reached down and plucked the thumbtack from the base of his neck. He briefly rubbed the stiffness from his shoulders and stood up to leave quietly. As he went to walk past Misty, she quickly reached out and grabbed him by the bloodstain on the front of his shirt. The movement was so quick that it startled Crystal and Julius. Misty pulled his face in close to hers and asked him, "What's your name, Captain Ahab?"

Julius looked down at his feet and softly uttered, "Lisa."

With that, Misty and Crystal were sufficiently sure that Julius would no longer be a problem, and Crystal was truly released from the whole terrible ordeal once and for all.

It had been a mentally and emotionally taxing evening for Crystal, and she hugged Misty a dozen times, thanking her for what she had done. The pair turned in an hour or so later, exhausted. Crystal fell asleep immediately. Misty, however, lay awake lost in thought just a little while longer.

If not for the scheduling conflict, Misty would have moved out the night before, and Crystal would have faced her attackers alone. She might have lost her friend forever, having no idea where to look for her and how help her. She would not have even been here to get to know Crystal had she not nearly lost her own life in the first place. She was hurt badly but had healed just enough to be able to respond to the attack this evening. Was it possible that what happened to her had purpose in the fact that she was able to be here to protect Crystal? Her mind twisted these possibilities over and over until she finally drifted off to sleep.

Both women slept better that night than either of them had in a very long time.

CHAPTER 17
Sharing in the Suffering

Unlike with Crystal, Craig had shared everything he knew about Misty's story with Paul.

It was about 10:00 p.m. when Craig and Misty arrived at Paul and Julianna's house. Julianna was tired from her chemo treatments and had gone to bed around 8:00 p.m. Craig explained to Misty that he had filled Paul in on her story because of all the connections he had, and that he felt Paul would be a great resource in finding her attacker and sorting out the legal problems of the guards at the Clandestine she had assassinated. He jokingly added, "All the murders before those are yours to sort out." Misty smiled lightly but was lost within herself. She was supposed to have been dropped off at Paul's house the night before. If that had happened, she would not have been at Crystal's house when her former pimp, Julius, had caught up with her. Who knows what horrors Crystal might be experiencing right now had she not been there to intervene? She had lost herself lately in this teaching job and had almost forgotten that she was a professional killer. She had crossed a line when she visited Pete's dad. She let her emotions get the best of her, and as a result, it nearly killed her. Everything had always seemed so clear to her, but now she was trapped inside herself and had no idea who she was or what to do.

She liked Pastor Craig. Over the years, she had met many men who were considered to be leaders. Of those, she had never encountered a man like him. His strength was evident but somehow otherworldly. She frequently observed the way he worked through each course of action. Whether it was a school problem, a counseling need, or a bloody professional killer showing up at his doorstep, he had a calm and rational response that sprang from that otherworldly confidence and strength. She was so lost in thought that she did not notice Craig had spoken to her.

"Misty?"

"Sorry…yeah."

"A penny for your thoughts?"

She had heard him say that phrase a few times. He could tell when a person was trapped inside themselves, and it was his way of encouraging them to let it out and talk. She trusted him, and decided to take advantage of their time alone in the car to release some of what she was struggling with. She responded very plainly, "So there was a situation last night."

With that, she relayed the whole story to Craig about the previous night's events. She also shared a little about the identity crisis she was experiencing. Her thoughts rolled out of her like a great flood, and before long she had to cut herself short because they had pulled up in Paul's driveway. Craig cut off the car and pulled the keys out of the ignition. Before they got out of the car, Craig looked over at Misty and let out some thoughts of his own.

"Look, Misty, I don't know what you think or believe about these things, but I am certain now that God has connected you to us. We each have to come to Christ in the context of the lives we have lived. He speaks to us through our experiences. I only know a very small portion of what you have experienced, but it is obvious that God has already used the skills you possess to be in the right place, at the right time, to save Crystal's life. I know you as a history teacher, not a professional killer. But Christ uses you as both, and that is the great mystery about you that I have wrestled with. If I have learned anything over the years in my relationship with God, it is to not ask so many questions. I know he has a plan and purpose for you. I know that you are conflicted right now inside yourself about these things. I would advise you to just quiet yourself for a while and wait to see what God does. You see, the other thing I have learned is that if we can slow ourselves down enough to really look for him, he always shows up."

She thanked him, and they both got out of the car and headed to the front door of Paul's house.

As they entered, Paul hugged Craig and reached out to shake Misty's hand. He had been trying to learn to speak Chinese for a few months and decided to try a greeting on Misty. It was off slightly, but Misty smiled and appreciated his effort. She repeated the greeting to him with the proper emphasis. Paul repeated the phase again, but this time correctly, and thanked her.

"I have been trying to learn Chinese for a couple months now. It will be my fourth language if I can pick it up. Come on in and have a seat." He led the way into their living room. It was a modest house considering the wealth Paul had acquired. It was modestly decorated, and Misty was pleasantly surprised that it was not what she had expected. Paul told them that Julianna had gone to bed worn out a couple hours ago but that she looked forward to a report about her class over breakfast. Craig asked about the chemo treatments and if the doctors knew whether or not she was responding to them, but they didn't have any answers yet.

Craig started the conversation. "Tell Paul what happened last night."

Paul listened intently as Misty relayed the events of the previous night. Paul looked over at Craig frequently throughout the tale in shocked disbelief. When she finished telling the story, Paul was temporarily speechless. It was clear that God had intervened on Crystal's behalf. It was astounding when he considered the series of events that had transpired in his own life that had caused him to have to bump things ahead by one day. He was actually frustrated at the time because he so diligently scheduled his time. When things did not go "according to plan" he was always off balance about it. In this moment, he decided to be a little less perplexed when things did not fit his schedule. You never know what God might be doing.

"Well, I guess I will give Crystal a big hug the next time I see her."

Paul motioned for Craig to hang out for a minute while he showed Misty to the guest room. Julianna had guessed at her size and had bought Misty a couple of sets of night clothes and a couple of outfits for during the day. They were lying on the bed in the guest room. Paul encouraged her to settle in and make herself comfortable.

"I have a full gym down in the basement that you are welcome to use in your recovery. If she feels up to it in the morning, Julianna will probably want to talk your ears off. We tell each other everything and keep no secrets. She knows what Craig and I know, but you can trust her to keep quiet as well. Maybe at some point in time you can help me with this Chinese?"

Misty thanked him in Chinese with a slight wink and then settled in.

Paul walked back out to the living room and motioned that he wanted to walk Craig out to the car. He was busting to talk to him now, but not where Misty might hear the conversation. When they got out to the driver's side of the car, Paul said with a chuckle, "Can you believe that!"

Paul was Craig's best friend and brother in the Lord. They met once a week for accountability and were brutally honest with each other. They also talked frequently throughout the week and helped each puzzle through whatever difficulties they each might be working through. Craig had shared many times with Paul that there was something hidden and subtle about Misty he could not pinpoint. He confided this to Paul because he wanted to be sure that his thoughts about her were not impure and that they were true speculations based on small quirks he had picked up on.

"I know, right! She shared the story with me on the way over in the car. Talk about right place at the right time." Craig did his best to speak quietly, but neither of them could believe the events surrounding Misty's arrival into their lives and how things had turned out.

"You were right again, brother! You called it! You have felt something was off about her for some time now. This definitely raises some interesting questions about the mysterious ways that God can use a person. Man, I hate to think about what might have happened to Crystal had Misty not been there. I can just imagine what went through Crystal's head when she realized that Julius had found her but that her new friend sitting there was an assassin… Wow!"

Craig replied, "The crazy thing is that I don't think of her as a killer, I still think of her as a history teacher. It's like my mind can't even put her there. Like it's not real. She is really wrestling with it as well. She told me that she has lost herself so much in this teaching job that she almost forgot that she is an assassin. It is like killing is what she has done, but she is questioning whether or not an assassin is what she is. It hurts my brain to think about how God might use a person with her skill set."

They both stood there and quietly considered that last statement for a few moments. They shook hands one last time, and then Craig jumped in the car to head home. Paul watched him pull away and stood outside for a few moments in the cool night air. It was an interesting thought to consider. There was no denying that Christ positioned Misty in the right time and place to protect Crystal. At the same time, if you spoke in church circles on the idea that Christ could use an unsaved assassin as part of his plan, you would get laughed out of the building. Paul pondered these things as he went back into the house to turn in. He chuckled to himself as he locked the door, thinking he really did not need to.

If anyone broke in…there was a professional killer in the house.

Misty awakened the next morning to the scent of coffee and bacon. The cast on her leg caused a maddening itch when she woke up every day. At times, the throbbing from the healing of her broken shin bone also seemed unbearable. She took a few moments before she got out of bed to meditate, control her breathing, and push out the pain. Technically, she should have been using crutches, but she refused to use them because she wanted her hands to be free. Dr. Robbins wasn't sure how that would affect her healing. It was difficult for him to set the broken bone without an x-ray as well. He figured she would most likely wind up with a limp the rest of her life for her troubles. Misty had developed the ability to quiet herself over the years though and was confident that through meditation she could ignore any pain and heal faster. Once her cast was taken off, she had Paul's gym downstairs at her disposal. She was confident that her recovery would not take long. Once she no longer felt the itch or the pain, she rolled out of bed and hobbled out to have breakfast with Julianna.

Misty was not prepared for how bad Julianna looked when she got to the kitchen. It must have registered on her face because Julianna smiled and said, "It's worse than it looks." While Misty was positioning herself over the nearest kitchen char, Julianna walked over to her and gave her a big hug. "Well, your life has taken some interesting turns lately."

"You have no idea…"

Julianna set a cup of coffee and a plate with bacon, eggs, and a couple pieces of buttered toast on the table in front of her. "It sounded so good to me when I started making it, but once it was done cooking, I was like…yuck. My appetite is weird these days." She took a seat across the table from Misty and poured herself a small cup of coffee. She looked pale and carried herself like she might shatter into a thousand pieces at any moment. The one thing that did not change was the beautiful sparkle of her eyes. In spite of how badly her body looked, her face lit up with her characteristic glow. Misty quickly scarfed down her breakfast. It was delicious. The pot of coffee was on the table between them. Julianna waited for her to finish eating and refill her cup before she broke the silence. "So you haven't killed any of the kids yet?"

Misty genuinely laughed at that comment. In fact she nearly spit coffee all over the table. "Believe me, the thought had crossed my mind a couple times."

Julianna laughed for the first time she had in a long time. They sat at the table for about an hour and caught up on history lessons and how the kids were doing. Pete, of course, came up in the conversation. Misty did not tell Julianna about her visit to see Pete's dad but happily reported the apparent change in his life and how it reflected through Pete. It was good news.

Julianna suggested they move to the living room and more comfortable seating. Misty told her to go ahead and cleared the table. Julianna had a million questions she wanted to ask Misty. She didn't want to be rude and pry if Misty wasn't ready to talk. She had made peace within herself that if cancer was going to take her out, then she was going to just live up until the day it happened with no regrets. When Misty joined her in the room and got seated, she decided life was too short to not attempt the conversation.

"I don't mean to be rude, and forgive me if I am being too personal, but how does a person wind up being a professional killer?" When she thought of an assassin, which was not very often, she pictured a big burly man. The fact that this stunningly beautiful woman sitting across from her in the room was a killer obviously did not make sense to her. The curiosity of how this came to be was fascinating.

Misty answered, "It is all I have ever known. As far back as I can remember, I lived in the facility and was trained to do it since I was a little child. Of course, the training was game based, and it was not until I was older that I discovered what the purpose of those games were."

Julianna listened quietly as Misty described the training she endured through her childhood. As Misty unloaded the brokenness of her life to Julianna, her heart was broken for Misty, She realized that she had no family and that because of her upbringing, it would be so difficult for her to experience the kind of love you can only get in the context of having a family. Misty shared with Julianna for a few hours and answered any questions that she asked. As they talked, it occurred to Misty that in spite of the toll the sickness and chemotherapy was having on her body, Julianna's spirit was still peaceful and joyful. She smiled and spoke with her characteristically soft tone as if there was nothing wrong. Misty finally had to ask her about it. "Can I ask you a question now?"

"Sure," Julianna replied

"We have been sitting here talking for a few hours. Honestly, I can clearly see that you are in pain or at least very sore. But you seem like it isn't bothering you at all. I have heard that chemotherapy can be brutal, but if you are suffering, a person could not tell by talking to you. How is that possible?"

Julianna answered her question with a question of her own, "Your shin bone was broken in two. Even though your leg is in a cast, it still has to be painful. I know for a fact that you are not taking pain pills for that pain. How is that possible?"

Misty answered, "Pain is in the mind. I have trained my mind through meditation to block out the pain. I simply shut it out or ignore it and push through it."

Julianna asked her, "Does your meditation work for your emotional pain as well?"

This was an unexpectedly difficult question to answer at first. Misty had been tormented lately and confused. It was true that she could block out physical pain, but it was getting increasingly difficult for her to deal with the feelings recent events had awakened inside her. She had to be honest with Julianna and herself. "No."

Then it was Julianna's turn to unload.

"Being diagnosed with cancer has helped me develop this theory. I think that we are never closer to Christ than we are when we are suffering. Think about it. Christianity teaches that God, the creator of all things, loved humanity enough that he came as a man and lived among us to teach us how live with him. He experienced everything that we do, but more. As Jesus, he could look into people. He could literally feel all our pain and infirmities. He could see the capacity in us for evil. He saw how easily the enemy could manipulate us with counterfeits of all the great things he has given us. A day of suffering will do more to build character in us than months of easy living. Suffering turns our hearts and minds toward God. It teaches us how frail we are and puts us in a place where we need to decide at a gut level whether or not we want to live or die. Because he loves us, when we are suffering, he suffers with us. He is actually present in our suffering. The fact that in my suffering I can know that he loves me and that he is present with me in it...*that* is how I can keep my joy and push through it."

Julianna's words touched Misty in a place she had never been touched. In her mind, she went back to when she was lying on the floor of her apartment, about to be killed. That was the lowest point she could remember in her entire life. She nearly gave up. In the physical and emotional pain in that moment, she did the only thing she could think to do. She called out to Jesus. It was not until later at Craig's house that she realized that Christ had been with her in that moment. What Julianna said was true; he was present in her suffering. She did not even consider herself to be a Christian. She had never made a decision concerning her spiritual path. None of this mattered. He was there with her anyway. She had heard Craig speak about Christ as if he was a person who was familiar to him. She was surrounded by people who talked about Christ the same way. Was it possible that God had caused her to be connected with these people so that he could reach out to her in this moment? If Christ was really reaching out to her through this whole series of events, what would happen if she tried to reach back? She decided to ask Julianna.

"That is beautiful. All of you at Thicker Than Water talk about Jesus like he is someone that you actually know. Can I know Jesus in the same way that all of you do? Is there a way that I can be sure he is present with me?"

Julianna smiled and said, "All you have to do to start with is reach out to him in faith and say a simple prayer. With that prayer, you acknowledge that you recognize now that he has been reaching for you and that you want to reach back. You give your heart to him."

She had nothing to lose in this moment. Things had spun wildly out of control for her. Everything seemed to be pointing to this moment and the decision she was about to make. She asked Julianna, "Can you teach me this prayer?"

Julianna crossed the room, took Misty by the hands and led her in the Sinner's Prayer.

And just like that, a woman who, from childhood, knew nothing but a lifetime as a professional killer became a child of God. Her situation did not change, her shin bone did not miraculously heal, but she moved from death unto life. Her story unknowingly changed. She activated a power in her life that would change everything. She would see now just how much Christ had been present with her. There is no such thing as coincidence in the kingdom of God.

Julianna explained to her that although she might not feel any different in this moment, this was a life-changing decision she had just made. She assured her that Christ was present with her and that she would now begin to see him in ways she never could before.

Paul came home and walked in to see them chatting intensely in the living room. He asked what they had been up to all day, and Julianna told him what had happened. Paul hugged Misty and congratulated her. Then he told her that he had connected with his friend Bill who used to be a pretty high-ranking military official. He was on the way over to see if he could help.

CHAPTER 18

Connections

At the sight of Bill standing right there in front of her, Misty suddenly had a moment of clarity concerning the connection of all the things she had experienced over the last few months. Her eyes welled with tears; she fell to her knees and began sobbing uncontrollably.

Bill was surprised by the reaction of this woman and had no idea who she was at first. He had not seen Misty since she was a little girl. Paul had been very vague with him on the phone about this new friend of his and some trouble she had gotten herself into. He had mentioned that the woman was Chinese, so Bill figured it was probably some easily resolved immigration issues. Paul and Julianna were also surprised at Misty's reaction. There was no way the three of them could understand what had overtaken her without an explanation. Julianna walked over to Misty, knelt down, put an arm around her, and said, "Misty, what's wrong?"

It was at that moment that Bill realized who this woman was. "Wait… Misty?"

Through the stream of tears in her eyes, Misty looked up at Bill and nodded her head to affirm her identity. When Bill finally understood who she was, his eyes welled with tears. He walked over to her, scooped her up into his arms, and hugged her tightly up against his chest. Her sobs turned to absolute wailing at that moment, and Bill also began to cry softly as well. Paul and Julianna still had no idea what was going on in their living room. They were touched and somehow knew that God had just done something unprecedented in their midst. It was about fifteen minutes before things quieted. It was Bill who spoke first.

"What trouble have you gotten into now, kid?"

Misty laughed heartily and wiped the tears from her eyes. "You have no idea."

Paul couldn't take it any longer and spoke up. "How do you two know each other?"

Misty collected herself and answered, "William was my mentor early on in my training. I have not seen him since I was, like, eight years old. He used to talk to me about Jesus, and he made a huge impression on me. Some of his lessons still stick with me today. I woke up one day and he was gone. I always wondered what happened and why he left, but they would never tell me." Misty paused, and then asked him, "Why did you leave me, William?"

William briefly explained, "I always had a problem with the agency training a child to be a professional killer. I argued constantly with my superiors about the moral and ethical implications of their secret program. Ultimately, they forced me to take an early retirement, with pay and benefits, under the threat of ruining my career if I didn't take the offer. It happened very suddenly, and I was not allowed to have any more contact with you. They felt my influence over you was counterproductive to your overall training."

Bill added some sarcasm to that last statement. All four shared a light chuckle about it.

Julianna suggested they all have a seat, and because of the warmhearted reunion she had just witnessed, she found the energy to go to the kitchen and get some drinks. Paul followed her into the kitchen to help and suggested to Misty that she fill Bill in on her situation.

Misty started her story from the last time she saw William. She had no family, and William had been the closest thing she ever had to a father. Paul and Julianna rejoined the two and distributed glasses of iced tea. They sat and listened to Misty as she told William of her travels and the assignments she had been given. She recounted details of elaborate plans, exotic locations, and brutal assassinations. The stories flowed from her like floodwaters that had broken through the pile of sandbags that were meant to hold them back.

As Julianna listened, she felt compassion. She could hardly believe that the woman who had taken over as substitute teacher of her history class had such a long history of killing people. Misty was alone in the world, and before that class, all she had was her work. She lost herself in the moment pondering what emotional struggles Misty might have been going through as she became inevitably more attached to the kids in that class. Word had gotten back to her that under Misty's instruction, test scores in that class were at an all-time high. It was clear that she had a natural gift for teaching. It would be a tragic loss to the kids, as well as the school, if Misty were hauled away in handcuffs for her crimes. But Misty had left a trail of bodies to answer for that spread all over the world and came to a head just outside the front of the Clandestine Hotel. It was clear that God had brought Misty to Thicker than Water Ministries, and Julianna just hoped she lived long enough to see what his ultimate purpose for that was.

As Paul listened, all he could think about was the previous night at Crystal's house. Julius could have dragged her away and back to the dreadful life she had escaped from. Had his flight not been delayed, he would have been home a day sooner, and Misty would have been at his house rather than Crystal's apartment. He had been so angry about that flight delay, mostly because he hated to be away from Julianna with the condition she was in. He never considered that God might work through something as mundane as a flight delay. More than that was the larger epiphany of the fact that God had strategically planted a trained killer in Crystal's apartment the night Julius happened to catch up to her. It was mind-boggling to think about the fact that God would choose to incorporate a trained killer in his plan, but that truth was undeniable now. Was it possible that God used anyone in the world he wanted to in order to accomplish his plan and that he was not limited merely to his followers? These events had Paul's theology all jacked up, and he knew as he listened to Misty that he was going to have to rethink some long-held opinions he had about God. All this was nothing compared to the startling reunion he had just witnessed in his living room. He couldn't wait to see Craig the next day and tell him about it. The overwhelmingly interesting question now burning in Paul's mind was how did Bill figure into all this?

Bill listened carefully to Misty's stories. He memorized locations and broke in whenever he could to ask for specific names for the secret missions she had been used for. A plan had already begun to form in his mind for a course of action to take. It was a long shot, and he made sure to note whatever details he could that would help. He hated to abandon Misty all those years ago. He took the forced retirement, but had always felt bad about doing it. He took advantage of the contacts he had made in different parts of the world to plan vacations for people wanted to travel. He made a decent amount of money doing that for a while, and started doing research toward investing some of it. As it turned out, he was decently gifted in the area of investments and finances, and that is how he made his living. He enjoyed doing the work and helping people reach their financial goals. He had also built up a considerable amount of power and influence through contributions to the political campaigns of some of his old military friends. Through it all, he still thought of Misty from time to time and prayed for her. That was the one wrong that continued to nag him, and he had sworn to himself over the years that if he ever had the chance to make it right, he would. As he continued to listen to Misty, his plan fell into place.

*****

In more ways than one, Misty had finally found her father.

It was totally lost on her that she was spilling long-lost military secrets. She had no concern that she was putting everyone in the room in mortal danger because of the top-secret nature of the stories she was telling. To Misty, it was no different than a high school girl telling her daddy about the wonderful time she had at the senior prom. The air seemed to be slowly sucking out of the room for Bill, Paul, and Julianna as they listened to her. As they continued to listen, her enthusiasm somehow became infectious. They began exchanging glances at each other across the room at first to share the occasional uneasy smile. After a little bit longer, the uneasiness gave way to a few light chuckles. At that point, Misty was saying something about a small town near Brazil, but she seemed to wake up into the situation and stopped speaking for a moment. She looked at the three of them with a puzzled look, as if she was trying to figure out what she had said that was funny—like she was the only person in the room that didn't get the inside joke. At this, the three of them burst out laughing. Bill finally got himself under control enough to speak up.

"Misty, sweetheart, you have just been telling us forbidden military secrets and stories about assassinations as if it was just normal everyday life. Although it has been for you, what you have been through is not normal. We were all just kind of taken aback by the ease of which you were telling your story. Why don't you skip ahead to who you think it might have been that finally caught up to you? Is there anything you can remember about that night?"

The room settled back down, and Misty jumped ahead in her story to the details of that night. She had given it a considerable amount of thought and decided that it was most likely the man Miller from the Clandestine hit that had somehow caught up to her. She had no idea how but given her ability to erase her tracks as she moved around the world, he was really the only possibility. She had decided that Miller was the first person she was going to look into once she had healed completely. The four of them talked about that possibility amongst themselves and decided that he was the most likely person. Bill and Paul agreed to look into who Miller was and see what they could find out about him. Bill also added that he had a few ideas concerning the hit at the Clandestine and how it might be cleaned up a little. He had to go see a couple people in person though and had to wait until the next day. They all decided that it was best for Misty to lie low. As they brought the night to a close, Paul suggested that Bill say a closing prayer for guidance and direction. By now, even Misty sensed that God was somehow at work in this whole situation. She had no idea how to pray, so she listened to Bill intently as he brought the evening to a close.

"Lord Jesus, this is an intense situation that we all have found ourselves in. I want to begin by thanking you for giving me the opportunity to right a wrong that has bothered me for a very long time. I see clearly now that you live inside of me and that the concerns of my heart are your concerns as well. Even now, you have already placed the seed of an idea within me toward resolving some of the issues we are facing. We count on your influence over the right people as this story unfolds. Please guide us and direct us in this situation. Show us your hand in ways that we can all point to and see as you being directly involved, and we will give you praise."

With that, Bill hugged the three of them and left. He had a decided on a course of action and promised he would call in a day or two once he saw how things played out. Paul showed him out and returned to Misty and Julianna in the living room. He looked at Misty and said, "So…about that small town near Brazil…"

CHAPTER 19
Loose Ends

Senator Grooms was a good man, but he was always a little bit late getting to his office in the morning. He was never a morning person, and he discovered that he could actually get more work done in the early evening after most people went home at the end of the day.

Bill showed up at his office bright and early at 8:00 a.m. He and Sam knew each other from all the way back in Army basic training. They were good friends. Their careers had taken them in different directions, but they had stayed in touch over the years. Bill had recently opened an office to work out of downtown which allowed for the two of them to meet for lunch frequently as well. He knew Sam would be in a little late, but wanted to catch him first thing before other work took hold of him. This also gave him the chance to hang out with Bridgette and chat for a little bit. Bridgette was Sam's receptionist and administrative assistant and probably one of the most beautiful women in the world. Most men became like melted butter in her presence. She had plush long blonde hair and great big blue eyes. She was very intelligent and had an outstanding bubbly personality. Bill had helped her and her husband work out a budget plan a couple years back, and it really opened up some things for them financially. She thanked him every time he visited. When he rounded the corner and entered the office lobby, she smiled widely at him.

"Billy!" She trotted out from behind her desk and gave him a big hug. Bill noticed that she had acquired a deep sun tan since he last saw her. He asked her about it as she released from her hug.

"Been getting a little sun?"

Bridgette answered him as she returned to her desk. "My husband and I just got back from a two-week vacation in Cancún. We never would have been able to do it without your help with our budget. We had a great time!" Bill nodded in approval. She continued, "Sam just called me. He should be in any minute." Bill took a seat and chatted with Bridgette about her vacation, and Sam showed up about ten minutes later.

"Bill, how are you doing?"

Bill moved toward him and shook his hand. "Pretty good, Sam. Actually, if you have some time this morning, I have a pretty big favor to ask."

Sam motioned for Bill to step into his office and opened the door for him. "Bridgette, please hold my calls for now."

Sam had a sitting area in his office. There were two high-backed leather chairs there with a small end table between them. Sam asked if Bill wanted anything to drink, and Bill declined. This seeming sense of urgency was out of character for Bill, and Sam wondered what the occasion was. He motioned for Bill to sit with him in the less formal sitting area rather than at the desk. Once they were seated, Sam asked, "What can I do for you, Bill?"

Bill started by saying, "Sam, I had a long and distinguished career with the military. For the most part, I enjoyed the work I did there. However, there was one program I was involved in that has troubled me all these years." Bill shared with Sam about Misty's training from childhood and the real story behind the reason for his retirement from the military. He shared that he swore to himself that if he could ever right that wrong, he would do whatever it took. Sam listened intently, and when Bill finished, he just shook his head and replied, "Wow, I had no idea."

Bill replied, "After all these years, Misty reached out to me for help last night." He explained about the hit that failed at the Clandestine Hotel as well as the events leading up to last night. Sam was amazed by this story, and at the same time, he understood the governmental storm it would create if the details of it were ever made public. Bill told him about the peace she had found as a teacher at

Thicker Than Water. Sam knew about the ministry. That pastor was doing some amazing things in the community, and after seeing the recent news story about it, he had decided to schedule a visit to the facility. Sam listened to everything Bill had to say and, when he was finished, asked him, "So what do you need from me old friend?"

Bill answered, "Well, the quiet solution to this is a full presidential pardon for any crimes Misty committed up to today here in the States. The not-so-quiet solution is that I prepare a statement about these things and release them to the media. You are my friend, Sam, and I hate to put you in a difficult position with this, but I have a chance to get this burden off my conscience. I have grown tired of carrying the weight of it."

Sam reassured Bill that he understood and said, "Sit tight for a moment, and let me make a couple calls." He walked over to his desk, paged Bridgette, and said, "Could you please see if you can get one of the president's people on the line? And tell them it's urgent."

While Sam was on the phone, Bill took a moment to walk over to the bookshelves on the other side of the room. His theory was that you can learn a lot about a person by seeing what kind of books they had on their bookshelf. Buying a book is an intentional act. At the very least, you can get a handle on a person's interests. There were two large shelving units in Sam's office. Most of the books were law or government related. A few titles jumped out at Bill as interesting books he might want to read himself. Sam had a copy of *Leadership Secrets of Attila the Hun* by Wes Roberts. He also had *Alternate Realities* by Dr. Lawrence Leshan. Both of these were compelling titles, and Bill made a mental note to check them out later. Sam was on the phone for about thirty minutes. When he called Bill to come back over and sit down, he seemed pretty confident.

"Well, I spoke to one of the president's aides. I gave them a couple names of the operations Misty allegedly was a part of. They have to do some research, of course, to make sure things are legitimate. They were appalled at the idea that our government would train a child to be a killer. That creates some real moral and ethical dilemmas. They told me to ask you for a couple days for research purposes and said that there will probably not be a problem getting what you asked for. They obviously want to keep a lid on this."

Bill shook Sam's hand and thanked him again. The two of them sat and took some time to catch up on other life events. Sam mentioned that at some point in time he wanted to meet Pastor Craig. He was really impressed with the impact his ministry was having on the community. Bill promised that whenever Sam had the time, he would make it happen. With that, the two parted company. Bridgette hugged Bill again when he left the office.

While Bill was walking back to his car, his cell phone rang. It was Paul calling. When he answered, Paul said, "You are not going to believe what I found out about this guy, Greg Miller!" Bill listened as he walked to the car.

"Miller was hired by Tony Ferrante for private security. The guards that Misty dispatched were actually employed by Miller. Miller filed bankruptcy because he could not afford to pay all the settlements to the guards' families. Misty said that Ferrante was the target of the hit and that he was supposed to be in the limo that day. Miller surprised her that day and nearly killed her, but she was able to drug him and get away. Miller lost everything, Bill. I think Misty might be right that it was him that attacked her. We have no idea how he found her though."

When Paul had finished, Bill only had one question. "So where is Miller now?

Once Miller had filed bankruptcy and moved out of his home, there was no current address for him. Bill thanked Paul for the call and said he would stop by his house the following evening with an update on the things he was working on. He still had a couple favors he could cash in on. He hung up from his call with Paul and dialed another number. After about an hour of phone calls and calling in favors, Bill had the address of Greg Miller's studio apartment. He was going to pay him a visit this evening, but he needed to stop at home first.

*****

165

It was late in the night, and Miller was fast asleep. He had been scouting at the school since his encounter with Misty and had not seen her. He was angry that she had gotten away that night. He had gotten caught up in the moment and mistakenly left her an opening. He would not repeat the mistake. He was pretty sure that she had gone into hiding. Surely there was no way she could trust anyone in church with her secret identity as an assassin. They would have turned her in immediately. He had looked in at her apartment a few times as well and far as he could see she had not been there since that night. It was frustrating to him that he had come so close and found her, but it seemed that he had lost her now. A strange feeling came over him while he slept. Over the years his sense of danger had served him well. Tired from work, Paul went straight to bed after getting home. He slowly awakened to another presence in the room with him. He was tired at first and tried to dismiss it, but as the minutes dragged on, he was increasingly sure of it. There was someone in the room. Without opening his eyes, he slowly reached for the pistol under his pillow.

A deep voice spoke to him from the darkness, "It's not there. Is *this* what you are looking for?"

Then he felt the cool metal barrel of his pistol pressed softly against the side of his head. He opened his eyes and saw the silhouette of a large man sitting in a chair beside his bed. He did not recognize the voice. He was totally hopeless. He did not know how long the person had been in the room with him, but they could have killed him already.

"So if you're not going to kill me, what do you want?" he asked.

The stranger continued, "You don't know who we are, Greg, but we know who you are. You came dangerously close to killing one of us a couple months ago. She will be fine, and you are lucky they sent me to talk to you rather than waiting for her to heal and come to see you."

Miller replied, "Razormist."

"Yes." The stranger continued. "Let this go, Greg. You are in way over your head here. If you are persistent, you might catch her again, you might even be able to kill her. But we are not the kind of people you want as your enemies Greg. We understand your desire for vengeance, but trust me, the little bit of vengeance you might get for this is nothing compared to the toll we will extract from your life for it. There is fifty thousand dollars in an envelope on the nightstand next to you. We encourage you to use it to move to another state and start a new life. You can take the money, or you can be found by the police here as an apparent suicide. My advice to you is to take the money and cut your losses."

Miller was angry. This dark stranger had the drop on him though, and he had no other options. The thought occurred to him that he could comply for now, and then he could take his chances later at finding and killing the woman.

As if this dark stranger could read his mind, he continued by saying, "Your hesitation suggests you might be thinking about taking our offer. Either that or maybe you take the money so I will leave and then continue this foolish agenda you have. Understand that we will never stop watching you. You will never see us, but we will always see you. When Razormist heals, we will keep her from seeking retaliation. You know she stays busy doing other things for us. *So* I will ask you one more time. Money? Or bullet?

Miller's eyes had adjusted to the dark enough that he could see the envelope on the nightstand. He slowly reached for it and pulled out the stack of bills. "I don't really have a choice, do I?"

"Not really."

Miller was tired. He had spent a lot of time trying to find and kill this woman. If what this stranger said was true, continuing this course of action was not worth the hassle. The juice was simply not worth the squeeze. So he agreed to the deal. He added, "I am going to have to break my lease on the apartment to leave now. I trust you will take care of that expense as well?"

The stranger affirmed that the lease would be covered and wished him good luck and a happy future. He had one more comment as he left the room.

"I will leave your pistol in the kitchen sink. Good night."

Miller heard the door close and figured the stranger was gone. He put the envelope back on the nightstand and rolled over to go back to sleep. He decided to try Florida.

*****

Bill removed his ski mask as he exited the apartment. It had been decades since he had done any black ops, and confronting Miller in this way made him briefly feel young again. He had enough money that the payoff he gave Miller would be barely noticeable. No one saw him coming or going. If things came through with Sam, he had effectively tied up any loose ends that would keep Misty from going back to the school. There was still the matter of the failed hit that might become a snag later, but for now the pressing problems would be resolved. No one needed to know that he personally confronted Miller. He could just say that he made some calls and that Miller would no longer be a problem. All these years, he had prayed for God to give him an opportunity to make this right. He slept better that night than he had in a long time.

CHAPTER 20
A Homecoming for Two

It rained hard the day Julianna died.

After all the prayers were offered up and in spite all the chemotherapy and radiation treatments, in the end, the cancer had just been too advanced before the doctors caught up to it. There is no rhyme or reason behind why good people die from cancer but bad people get to keep on living. Julianna was feeling particularly weak one afternoon and told Paul she needed to go take a nap. A few hours later, he went in to check on her and found her unresponsive. There was no nice bedside moment story to tell. No last words were uttered to a small group of important loved ones gathered around the room. Her last words were, "I love you. I need to go take a nap." Paul knew this day was coming and had prepared his heart for it. There was still an element of heartbreak, but he was fortunate to have had the privilege of being married to his middle school crush. She had repeatedly told him as well that he was not allowed to be sad when the Lord finally called her home. In her better moments the last few months, she told several people that there was to be no crying at her funeral and that she wanted it to be a celebration.

Paul called Craig and told him the bad news. Craig said that he and Kay would be there as soon as possible. The house seemed strangely quiet as he waited for people to arrive. He knew that strange quietness was something he was going to have to learn to live with for a while. Bill was the first to arrive. He hugged Paul tightly and asked him how he was doing.

"It just seems like an otherworldly quiet has settled over the house—like somehow when her spirit moved on, it left a weird vacuum in its absence." Bill nodded that he understood. Craig and Kay arrived about twenty minutes later. They both hugged Paul. Kay had tears in her eyes, and when she reminded Paul that nobody was supposed to cry, it was as much for her as it was for him. Two men arrived and started at the grim task of wrapping up Julianna's body and wheeling her out to the hearse. The four of them made some loose plans for how to move through the next couple days and talked about how to put together a fitting memorial service for her. Julianna passed away on a Wednesday evening. The decision was made to close the school until the following Monday. Julianna left her mark on the hearts of everyone around her. While some tears were definitely shed, most people were able to deal with the loss with a sense of joy and a bit of laughter because she insisted on it.

As opposed to the day she died, it was a beautiful sunny day for the funeral. Julianna's burial plot was at the top of a huge hill near the back of the cemetery. The view from that spot overlooked the great green grass and rolling hillsides beyond the back side of the fenced-in cemetery property. It was a fitting final resting spot for such a beautiful person. The cemetery driveway was packed on both sides, with all the cars that had come for the graveside service. One of the cemetery workers would later tell Paul, Craig, and Kay that it was the largest crowd they had ever seen there. The service only lasted a few minutes, but it was nearly an hour and a half before all the cars had cleared out from the property.

Misty could not help but be happy. She dearly missed Julianna, but she knew her pain had ended and that she was in a better place. It was Julianna that led her to the Lord several months ago. So much had happened since then it was hard to get a grip on all of it. It wasn't even an hour after she had said the prayer and accepted Christ that she was reunited with her childhood mentor, William. She had been recovering from injuries from an encounter with a man named Miller who had nearly killed her. Two days later, Bill had visited her at Paul's house to see how her recovery was going. While he was there, his cell phone rang. He answered the call and handed her the phone, telling her that the call was for her. It was the president of the United States! He was very nice to her, and she couldn't believe it was actually him at first. He apologized for the way "certain entities" had taken advantage of her since childhood. To reinforce that apology, he issued a full pardon for any and all crimes she had "allegedly" committed up to the day Bill first reached out to him. He reassured her that while killing might be what she had done, teaching was probably who she was and what her gift was to the world. He encouraged her to stay strong in her newfound faith and enjoy the rest of her years in peace and good health. She thanked him and promised she would do her best. She was on a high from that phone call for several days. Bill had also reassured her that Miller was "paid a visit," and that he would no longer be a problem. Julianna's eyes filled with tears that day, and she hugged Misty more tightly than she ever had before. For just a moment, it was as if there was no cancer and the healing in Misty's life had somehow spilled over as a physical healing for her. A week later, the cast was removed from Misty's leg, and she was free to go back to her teaching job at Thicker Than Water.

As Misty stood here on this hillside and listened to Craig read the words of Psalm 23, it was as if Julianna had become the sun and was shining on her from somewhere above.

> The Lord is my shepherd, I shall not want.
> He makes me lie down in green pastures;
> he leads me beside still waters; he restores my soul.
> He leads me in right paths for his name's sake.
> Even though I walk through the darkest valley, I fear no evil;
> for you are with me; your rod and your staff—they comfort me.
> You prepare a table before me in the presence of my enemies;
> you anoint my head with oil; my cup overflows.
> Surely goodness and mercy shall follow me all the days of my life,
> and I shall dwell in the house of the Lord my whole life long.

She looked at the crowd around her and realized something that brought warmth to her heart she had never felt before. Paul was here. He was smiling, but it was a bittersweet smile as he tried to figure out how he was going to live the rest of his life without his beloved Julianna. Kay was beside her husband as he delivered the final words of the graveside service closing prayer. They were a wonderful couple and were like a brother and sister to her now. As she continued scanning the crowd, she noticed that a man across the crowd had nodded at her. She didn't recognize him at first—at least not until she saw his son Petey standing by his side. Ralph was clean cut and had lost several pounds. His wife stood closely beside him, and he had his arm around her. With that nod, he seemed to communicate appreciation to her for helping to set him straight. She smiled lightly and nodded to him in return. In all this, she had found something she never had before…a family.

As broken as it was, this was her family. Wherever their lives touched, love was the result. She had been to a few funerals in her lifetime but had never sensed an attachment to people like she did here. Her life was entirely different now. As she continued to scan the crowd, her eyes rested to her new best friend standing right next to her. Crystal was her closest friend in the world. She was like the sister she never had. People had begun to leave, and Crystal had walked over to talk to Kay. In that moment, Misty had a sudden epiphany. There was something she had to do.

When the sleek sports car first pulled up in the driveway, Lydia happened to see it and wondered who would be pulling in the driveway, driving such a nice and expensive car. She opened the front door and started out to the porch, hollering behind her, "Someone is here, and they are driving the coolest car I have ever seen!" Deborah had been playing on her phone but got up to look out the front window. She was also impressed by the car and made her way to the door to see who this new visitor was.

Still inside the car, Misty looked at Crystal and said, "They are your family. You should have done this a long time ago. Now come on. Don't be ridiculous… Let's go." Misty opened her door and stepped out of the car first. Lydia and Deborah saw Misty exit the driver side of the car but had no idea who she was. Just as they were getting ready to greet her, the passenger door started to open. Crystal had seen her two sisters approaching the car. She took a deep breath and decided it was time to get out.

Lydia was the first to recognize her sister. She screamed, "OH MY GOD! CRYSTAL!" Lydia ran to her and jumped on her. The force was so hard it nearly knocked both of them on the ground. Both of them began sobbing uncontrollably. Deborah could not believe her eyes. She yelled into the house, "MOM! DAD! CRYSTAL IS BACK!" Then she sprinted over and joined her sisters' sobbing embrace. It was a few moments before Crystal's mom appeared on the porch. She stood in shock and disbelief for a few moments, like she could not believe her eyes. She was sobbing before she walked off the porch. She trotted over and hugged Crystal tightly.

By now, Misty had walked around to the front of the car and was propped up against the passenger-side fender, watching this happy reunion take place. She was glad she encouraged Crystal to do it. Crystal had apprehensions about going back to her family because she was ashamed about what had happened to her. She had no idea how to explain all of it to her family. Misty had recently begun to understand the importance of family. She assured Crystal that none of that mattered and that she was sure that her family missed her and would want to know that she was okay. This tear-filled reunion was proof that she was right. Crystal's mother and sisters cried and hugged Crystal and looked her over as if they could not believe she was actually standing there.

The most difficult person in Crystal's mind to come home to was her father. She told Misty that she could not keep herself together under her father's cold religious gaze. When he finally appeared from inside the house on the front porch, Misty was not impressed. Crystal's sisters and mother, all three, turned away from her and looked toward her father to see what his reaction was going to be. There was an awkward pause in that moment, as if the entire world silenced itself to see what would happen next.

Crystal slowly met her dad's gaze, but what she saw there surprised her. It was not the cold religious gaze that had intimidated all her life. The hard religious zeal had been replaced with something else. With tears in his eyes, he walked slowly to Crystal, wrapped his arms around her, and said "Welcome home."

The five of them hugged and cried, and the family still seemed to stare occasionally at Crystal in disbelief that she was actually standing there. It was like she had come back from the dead. It was Crystal's mom who seemed to suddenly notice Misty standing nearby. She walked over to her and introduced herself. "Hi, I am Linda, Crystal's mother. Who are you?"

Misty replied, "I am a good friend of Crystal's. My name is Misty." Misty extended a hand out toward her to shake her hand. Crystal's mother stepped closer to her, gently pushed her hand out of the way, and hugged Misty tightly. She whispered softly to her, "Thank you for bringing my baby home to me." Misty nodded to her as she stepped away.

Now the rest of the family seemed to take notice of Misty. Crystal said, "Guys, this is my best friend Misty. We have been through a lot together. She saved my life, and I would probably not be here if it wasn't for her." Lydia immediately walked over and hugged Misty. Deborah also walked over and hugged her. Both sisters thanked her for saving their sister's life and bringing her home. Crystal's dad slowly walked over and extended a hand to Misty as if he was going to shake her hand. When Misty took hold of his hand to shake it, he pulled her in for a hug as well. He said, "Thank you for bringing Crystal back to us. We have not heard from her in years and thought she was dead. You have no idea of the blessing you have brought to my house today."

Crystal's mother asked how long their journey was and asked Misty if she could stay for dinner. It was a Friday evening, and Crystal said if it was okay with everyone, they would both be staying for the weekend. There was a lot of catching up to do. Of course, this was met with enthusiastic agreement from everyone, and the family headed inside. Misty suggested they go ahead of her and that she would be inside in a minute once she got the travel bags out of her trunk. Once they were all inside, Misty took a moment to stand outside and reflect.

She remembered Julianna telling her when she accepted Christ that her life was going to change in ways she could never imagine. There was so much left to figure out. But her quality of life had improved so much in the last few months that she could not make sense of it. Today, she decided to just sit back and enjoy it. Before she went inside, she lifted a quick prayer because it felt right at the moment.

"Jesus, thank you for everything you have done. Thank you that today I can say you have changed me from Razormist to Misty. I have no idea what the future holds for me. But if it is okay with you, I am going to not think about that for now and just enjoy this moment. Thank you for love, and thank you for giving me a family. Oh yeah, and say hi to Julianna for me."

About the Author

Dennis McFarland grew up on the east side of Columbus, Ohio, and his parents still live in the house he was raised in. During his early adult years, he struggled through drug and alcohol addiction, anxiety, and depression. Through the vehicle of his spirituality, he found focus and purpose. He graduated from Ohio Christian University with two bachelor's degrees in 2009. Now he earns his living helping people to find their own focus and purpose. He started his website, www.ttwmtruth.com, in an attempt to combat negative Christian stereotypes through his writings and video sermons. He also started a podcast entitled *From the War Room* for that same purpose. Dennis currently lives in London, Ohio, with his wife, his son, and his best friend, his boxer Loki.